SIR ROBERT ANDERSON

The Thinking Man's Guide to the Bible

Gerald B. Shugart

Lulu Publishing | Morrisville, North Carolina

SIR ROBERT ANDERSON
The Thinking Man's Guide to the Bible

by

Gerald B. Shugart

Formatting conducted by ShelfBloom ePress. Concerns about formatting, typographical errors, etc. should be sent to support@shelfbloom.com

DEDICATION

This book is dedicated to my dear friends in Eldorado, Texas,
Bob and Nancy Lester, Richard and Jill Preston, Lynn and
Christy Meador, Rusty Meador, Ricky Jones, Mack McAngus
and my cousins Danell, Karl, Kyle and Cody McCormack, and
my other cousin, Larry Meador, whose roots are in Eldorado.

Special thanks to Jason P. Randolph, without whose
encouragement and patience my books would have never seen the
light of day.

TABLE OF CONTENTS

Chapter 1

Sir Robert Anderson - The Thinking Man

On March 20th of the year 1910, the residents of New York City were awakened to a headline in the *New York Times* which proclaimed:

The Truth at Last About Jack the Ripper

London Police Had Him in their Net But Couldn't Convict Him – Problems of the Criminal Insane

There can be little doubt that this headline attracted much attention as the Ripper case was the most sensational murder mystery of the time, being the subject of a global media frenzy. The article in the *Times* said:

"Sir Robert Anderson, for more than thirty years Chief of the Criminal Investigation Department of the British Government, and head of the Detective Bureau at Scotland Yard, has at length raised the veil of mystery which for nearly two decades has enveloped the identity of the perpetrator of those atrocious crimes known as the Whitechapel murders...Sir Robert establishes the fact that the infamous 'Jack the Ripper,' as the unknown slayer had been dubbed by the public, and at whose hands no less than

fourteen women of the unfortunate class successively lost their lives within a circumscribed area of the East End of London, was an alien of the lower, though educated class, hailing from Poland, and a maniac of the most virulent and homicidal type."

Later in the article more details of the case were revealed, including the facts of the suspect's detention:

"The most important point of all made by Sir Robert is the fact that once the Criminal Investigation Department was sure that it had in its hands the real perpetrator of the Whitechapel murders, it procured from the Secretary of State for the Home Department a warrant committing the man for detention 'during the King's pleasure' to the great asylum at Broadmoor five or six years ago."

The Ripper's name was Aaron Kosminski, and his arrest was the result of a house to house search by Scotland Yard in the area where the crimes took place. In Anderson's biography, written by his son Arthur Posonby Moore-Anderson, we read that Scotland Yard had no doubt that they had captured Jack the Ripper:

"Scotland Yard, however, had no doubt that the criminal was eventually found. The only person who ever had a good view of the murderer identified the suspect without hesitation the instant he was confronted with him; but he refused to give evidence. Sir Robert stated as a fact that the man was an alien from Eastern Europe, and believed that he died in an asylum." [1]

From the beginning of Anderson's appointment as Chief of the Criminal Investigation Department of Scotland Yard he was assigned the duty of solving the Whitechapel murder case. His son wrote:

"The 'Jack the Ripper' scare, resulting from the Whitechapel murders of the year 1888, synchronised with my father's appointment as Assistant Commissioner of Metropolitan Police and Chief of the C.I.D. For reasons of health he was ordered two months' complete rest before entering upon his duties, and after a

week at the Yard he left for the Continent. The second of the murders was committed the night before he took office and the third occurred during the night of the day on which he left London. The newspapers soon began to comment on his absence, and when two more victims had fallen to the knife of the murderer-fiend, an urgent appeal from the Home Secretary brought the new Chief back to duty. 'We hold you responsible to find the murderer' were the words which greeted him." [2]

Warren W. Wiersbe provides a synopsis of Anderson's career in law enforcement:

"Robert Anderson was born in 1841 in Dublin where his father, Matthew Anderson, served as Crown Solicitor for the city...In 1863 he (Sir Robert) was made a member of the Irish Bar and served on the legal circuit. About this time, the Fenians were at work (a secret society attempting to overthrow British rule in Ireland), and he became involved interrogating prisoners and preparing legal briefs. This was his introduction to police work. He was married in 1873 and four years later moved to London as a member of the Home Office staff. He had access to the detective department and made good use of it. In 1888, while Jack the Ripper was terrorizing London, Anderson moved into Scotland Yard as Assistant Commissioner of Metropolitan Police and Chief of the Criminal Investigation Department." [3]

Anderson's quick mind proved invaluable in his police work:

"An article in Black and White on 'The Detectives who Frustrated the Dynamite Plot' (in 1896) said : 'In Dr. Anderson's appearance there is more of the man of peace than of the terror of conspirators. Yet it is certain that he has been a conspicuous success in his high office, thanks to his analytical mind, his keen reasoning powers, and his scent for the right trail'...Another impression, given two years later, was: 'Dr. Anderson has been described and fitly as the ideal detective of real life, yet he bears but little resemblance to those of the novelists' creation. . . His power of close and rapid reasoning from facts and his marvellous quickness in seizing on the essential points in difficult cases are

3

at once the wonder and admiration of the men under his control. Naturally he is a discreet, silent and reserved man; his training has made him even more so, but no officer who has yet presided over the affairs of the C.I.D. can boast of being more popular or more genuinely respected by his subordinates.' " [4]

John Moylan, in his book titled *Scotland Yard and the Metropolitan Police,* stated that

*"The period 1890 to 1900 proved to be one during which there was almost continuous decrease in crime...By signal successes in sensational cases...and by steady achievement in the less advertised everyday business of dealing with rogues in general, the C.I.D. built up in the 'nineties' a world-wide reputation for efficiency in crime detection." * [5]

The period of Sir Robert Anderson's service as Chief of the Criminal Investigation Department was from 1888 until 1901. In 1896 Anderson was knighted by Queen Victoria and then upon his retirement from government service King Edward VII bestowed on him the further honor of Knight Commander. Anderson's success as an investigator resulted in others referring to him as *"the Prince of Detectives," "Super-Detective,"* and *"Secret Service Theologian."*

Sir Robert grew up in a devout Christian home and early in his life he was active as a lay preacher and he brought many to the knowledge of the Lord Jesus Christ. Wiersbe says that Anderson

*"Authored seventeen major books on Biblical themes...Charles H. Spurgeon said that Anderson's book 'Human Destiny' was 'the most valuable contribution on the subject' that he had ever seen. These books underscore the inspiration and dependable authority of the Bible, the deity of Jesus Christ, and the necessity of the new birth. He tracked down myths and religious error, arrested and exposed it, with the same skill and courage that he displayed when he tracked down criminals." * [6]

4

The following is a short sketch of Anderson's life as seen through the eyes of his son:

" 'AN anglicised Irishman of Scottish extraction.' My father's description of himself. Born in Dublin of Ulster stock, his youth was spent in the part of Ireland now known as Eire. Called to the Irish Bar he was early side-tracked into Secret Service work in connection with the Fenian movement of those times. When this led to his crossing the Channel to England it was, as he after-wards expressed it, with a return ticket in his pocket. But from that day his native land knew him only as a visitor. First in the Home Office, then at Scotland Yard, and finally in retirement, he remained a Londoner for the rest of his life. Duty made him a re-lentless tracker of criminals. But the dynamiters would have been more than a little surprised had they known that the man behind the scenes who hunted them down was author of many books on the Bible and the Christian life. No less amazed would have been many a professional burglar should he have come upon the C.I.D. Chief giving a Gospel address in some London mission hall. His life of seventy-seven years was a many-sided one, in some re-spects unique." [7]

Anderson applied the same investigative techniques which he had perfected during his career in the Secret Service and at Scotland Yard to his study of the Bible. During a time when many were questioning the authenticity of the book of *Daniel* Anderson wrote:

"Long accustomed to deal with evidence in difficult and intri-cate inquiries, I have set myself to investigate the genuineness of the Book of Daniel." [8]

John Phillips also wrote a book in the defense of the book of *Daniel* and in that book he quoted Anderson many times and says that Sir Robert was:

"In his day the respected head of Britian's prestigious Scot-land Yard. He was not only a well-taught Bible scholar with a number of thought-provoking books to his credit but also a man

well versed in interrogating witnesses, detecting falsehood, and exposing the sophistries of error." [9]

James M. Gray (1852-1935), who served for thirty years as President of Moody Bible Institute and was one of the seven editors of the original *Scofield Reference Bible*, said the following about Anderson:

"Sir Robert Anderson is in some respects the most remarkable of current writers on religious subjects, whether we consider his personal history or the range and character of his work...To sit at the feet of a man with such knowledge, mental power, courage and native wit, who is at the same time Spirit taught, is for the true Christian one of the greatest privileges." [10]

Warren Wiersbe wrote that *"if you have never met Sir Robert Anderson, then you are about to embark on a thrilling voyage of discovery. If he is already one of your friends, then finding a new Anderson title, or meeting an old one, will bring joy to your heart and enlightenment to your mind." [11]*

Sir Robert Anderson can indeed be described as a "Thinking Man," and this book will begin his "Guide to the Bible" with a study of the record of the progressive revelation which God has given to man and man's response to that revelation.

NOTES

1. A.P. Moore-Anderson, *The Life of Sir Robert Anderson* (London: Marshall, Morgan & Scott, 1947), 51.

2. *Ibid.*, 49.

3. Sir Robert Anderson, *Redemption Truths* (Grand Rapids: Kregel Publications, 1980), vi.-vii.

4. A.P. Moore-Anderson, *The Life of Sir Robert Anderson*, 60.

5. *Ibid.*, 62.

6. Sir RobertAnderson, *Redemption Truths*, viii.

7. A.P. Moore-Anderson, *The Life of Sir Robert Anderson*, 1.

8. Sir Robert Anderson, *Daniel in the Critic's Den* (Grand Rapids: Kregel Publications, 1990), x.

9. John Phillips, *The Book of Daniel: An Expository Commentary* (Grand Rapids: Kregel Publications, 2004), 225.

10. A.P. Moore-Anderson, *The Life of Sir Robert Anderson*, 95.

11. Sir Robert Anderson, *Redemption Truths*, viii.

Chapter 2

The Bible as a Whole

Sir Robert Anderson writes that the Bible is much more than a textbook of theology and morals:

"The Bible is far more than a textbook of theology and morals, or even than a guide to heaven. It is the record of the progressive revelation God has vouchsafed to man, and the Divine history of our race in connection with that revelation. Ignorance may fail to see in it anything more than the religious literature of the Hebrew race, and of the Church in Apostolic times; but the intelligent student who can read between the lines will find there mapped out, sometimes in clear bold outline, sometimes dimly, but yet always discernible by the patient and devout inquirer, the great scheme of God's counsels and workings in and for this world of ours from eternity to eternity." [1]

According to Anderson a study of "dispensational truth" is the key to understanding the hidden harmony of the divine scheme of the Bible:

"Holy Scripture had long been like an elaborate mosaic, of which the several parts had been disturbed, and the main design forgotten. But its hidden harmony was brought to light by the study of 'dispensational truth.' " [2]

He also says that the New Testament cannot be read intelligently until the Divine scheme and purpose of the Bible "as a whole" is first understood:

"The words of God are like the works of God, in that we often need the microscope to enable us to appreciate them. And yet at

times this element is of secondary importance. For, unless we understand the Divine scheme and purpose of the Bible as a whole, we cannot read even the New Testament intelligently." [3]

The Basics of Dispensationalism

Broadly defined, a "dispensation" is *"that which is distributed or given out."*

A Biblical Dispensation is something that is given out or dispensed by God and given to man. In the Scriptures the Greek word translated "dispensation" is *oikonomia* so in order to have a correct theological understanding of exactly what is dispensed to man from God we must know the meaning of that Greek word.

Joseph Henry Thayer defines *oikonomia* as *"the management of a household or of household affairs; specifically, the management, oversight, administration, of other's property; the office of a manager or overseer, stewardship."* [4]

Thayer also says that *"the word is transferred by Paul in a theocratic sense to the office (duty) intrusted to him by God (the lord and master) of proclaiming to men the blessings of the gospel, 1 Co. ix. 17..."* [5]

By its very nature a "stewardship" involves responsibilities and throughout the Bible we see God assigning various responsibilities to either individuals or groups of people. These various "dispensations" or "stewardships" are the ways by which God chooses to run the affairs of the household/world and they do not represent different ways of salvation. It could be said that the various dispensations are the different ways which God governs His creatures and thus the different dispensations represent the various governments of God.

Next we will examine the different dispensations which were assigned to men in their chronological order, beginning with the "Dispensation of National Service."

10

I. The Dispensation of National Service

God made a promise to Abraham, telling him that *"I will make of thee a great nation"* and *"in thee shall all the families of the earth be blessed":*

"Now the Lord had said unto Abram, Get thee out of thy country, and from thy kindred, and from thy father's house, unto a land that I will show thee; and I will make of thee a great nation...and in thee shall all families of the earth be blessed" (Gen.12:1-3). [6]

To put this promise into perspective Anderson says that the the Old Testament is the Divine history of the family of Abraham:

"Men talk of the Divine history of the human race, but there is no such history. The Old Testament is the Divine history of the family of Abraham. The call of Abraham was chronologically the central point between the creation of Adam and the Cross of Christ, and yet the story of all the ages from Adam to Abraham is dismissed in eleven chapters. And if during the history of Israel the light of revelation rested for a time upon heathen nations, it was because the favoured nation was temporarily in captivity. But God took up the Hebrew race that they might be a centre and channel of blessing to the world." [7]

The great nation which received the promise was Israel, and a stewardship was given to that nation that she should serve the Lord:

"...the oath which He swore to our Father, Abraham, that He would grant unto us that we, being delivered out of the hand of our enemies, might serve Him without fear, in holiness and righteousness before Him, all the days of our lives" (Lk.1:73-75).

The nation was to be a channel of blessing to the world, and one of the duties assigned to Israel was the stewardship to be a "witness" of God's existence and to the fact that there is only one God:

"Ye are my witnesses, saith the LORD, and my servant whom I have chosen: that ye may know and believe me, and understand that I am he; before me there was no God formed, neither shall there be after me. I, even I, am the LORD, and beside me there is no savior. I have declared, and have saved, and I have shown, when there was no strange god among you; therefore ye are my witnesses, saith the LORD, that I am God" (Isa.43:10-12).

Anderson next gives more details about Israel's "service":

"They were chosen, so to speak, to be the Divine agents upon earth, and 'unto them were committed the oracles of God' (Rom. iii. 2). Now in commerce an agent is appointed, not to restrict, but to facilitate, the supply of goods to the public; and also to ensure that they shall reach the public pure and unadulterated. And the Divine purpose in giving that position to the Covenant people, and 'committing to them the oracles of God,' was that the truth of God in its purity, and the blessings which accompany the knowledge of it, might be accessible to all mankind." [8]

Israel's ultimate purpose is stated as follows:

"Ye are the light of the world...Let your light so shine before men, that they may see your good works, and glorify your Father, Who is in heaven" (Mt.5:14,16).

After the Lord made these promises He began to fulfill them by giving Abraham many descendants. Not long after the children of Israel had settled into the land which God had given them they experienced a famine so they went into Egypt. There they were welcomed by the king who gave unto them the best of the land. They prospered and multiplied until they numbered about two million. Later, a different king succeeded the one who welcomed them and they were made slaves and forced to work from morning until night:

12

"The children of Israel sighed by reason of the bondage, and they cried, and their cry came up unto God...and God heard their groaning, and God remembered His covenant with Abraham" (Ex.2:24).

After this God chose Moses to deliver His people out of Egypt and out of their bondage, saying unto him:

"I will send thee unto Pharaoh, that thou mayest bring forth My people, the children of Israel, out of Egypt" (Ex.3:10).

The Lord then fulfilled His promise to Abraham that He would deliver Israel out of the hands of her enemies:

"But because the Lord loved you, and because He would keep the oath which He had sworn unto your fathers, hath the Lord brought you out with a mighty hand, and redeemed you out of the house of bondage, from the hand of Pharaoh, king of Egypt" (Deut.7:8).

After leading the children of Israel across the Red Sea and destroying the armies of Pharaoh the Lord also fought and destroyed the armies of Amalek in the wilderness (Ex.17:8-13). Even though the Lord had kept His promise the Israelites did not *"serve Him in holiness and righteousness."* Instead, they rebelled against Him:

"Remember, and forget not, how thou provoked the Lord thou God to wrath in the wilderness; from that day that thou didst depart out of the land of Egypt, until you came into this place, ye have been rebellious against the Lord" (Deut.9:7).

So, we can see that the children of Israel refused to serve the Lord in holiness and righteousness. Instead, they were rebellious and their behavior made it obvious that in their present state it would be impossible for them to be known among the Gentiles as *"the seed which the Lord hath blessed"*:

"And their seed shall be known among the Gentiles, and their offspring among the people: all that see them shall acknowledge

them, that they are the seed which the LORD hath blessed" (Isa.61:9).

II. The Dispensation of the Law

If the nation of Israel was ever going to fulfill her destiny as "the light of the world" it was now necessary for God to place that nation under "the law," and the law would serve as a "schoolmaster":

"Wherefore, the law was our schoolmaster to bring us to Christ..." (Gal.3:24).

The Greek word translated "schoolmaster" is *paidagogos*, and a *paidagogos* was a disciplinarian who was given the responsibility of giving children moral training and keeping them from the evils of the world. The Law was to act as a tutor in order to place the children of Israel under a strict discipline. The Law was the Divine religion of Judaism and Anderson writes:

"In the ages when His people were in a state of tutelage, God gave them a religion. It was a concession to the weakness of human nature." [9]

If the children of Israel would keep the Law (also known as the Mosaic Covenant) then she would be an "holy nation":

"If ye will obey my voice indeed, and keep my covenant, then ye shall be a peculiar treasure unto me above all people: for all the earth is mine: And ye shall be unto me a kingdom of priests, and an holy nation" (Ex.19:5-6).

If Israel would faithfully keep the Law then the other nations would know them as a wise and understanding people:

"Behold, I have taught you statutes and judgments, even as the LORD my God commanded me, that ye should do so in the land whither ye go to possess it. Keep, therefore, and do them; for this is your wisdom and your understanding in the sight of the na-

tions, who shall hear all these statutes and say, Surely this great nation is a wise and understanding people" (Deut. 4:5-6).

According to King Solomon all the people of the earth were to gain a knowledge of the one true God through Israel:

"The LORD our God be with us, as he was with our fathers: let him not leave us, nor forsake us: That he may incline our hearts unto him, to walk in all his ways, and to keep his commandments, and his statutes, and his judgments, which he commanded our fathers...that all the people of the earth may know that the Lord is God, and that there is none else" (1 Ki.8:57-58,60).

Anderson says the following about the words of King Solomon:

"The book has yet to be written which will describe what Israel might have been, and the world would have been, had the favoured nation been true to the revelation God entrusted to them. Solomon's prophetic prayer at the dedication of the temple gives a transient glimpse of the vision (1 Kings viii. and 2 Chron. vi.). Blessed with the knowledge of the true God in a world that had wilfully lost it, they would have been a rallying centre to which earnest souls of every kindred might have come to seek and find the light. Professing a sublime faith, and commending it by noble and blameless living, they would have been missionaries to all the nations." [10]

The Lord also revealed that the "the law" was both "a blessing and a curse":

"I set before you this day a blessing and a curse: A blessing, if ye obey the commandments of the Lord your God, which I command you in this day; And a curse, if ye will not obey the commandments of the Lord your God, but turn aside out of the way which I command you this day, to go after other gods, which ye have not known" (Deut.11:26-28).

God also promised King David that his son, Solomon, would build a Temple and the throne of his kingdom will be established forever:

"He shall build a house for My name, and I will establish the throne of his kingdom forever" (2 Sam.7:13).

At the dedication of the Temple that King Solomon built *"the glory of the Lord had filled the house of the Lord"* (1 Ki.8:11). Over time Solomon's kingdom exceeded all the other kingdoms of the earth:

"King Solomon exceeded all the kings of the earth in riches and for wisdom. And all the earth consulted Solomon, to hear his wisdom, which God had put in his heart" (1 Ki.10:23,24).

But Solomon went down to Egypt for his queen, the daughter of Pharaoh, who *"turned away his heart after other gods"* (1 Ki.11:1,4). As time passed the kingdom ruled by Solomon became a hindrance to God's purposes. Israel began to treat the Gentiles with contempt, and instead of revealing the true God to them, *"the name of God"* was *"blasphemed among the Gentiles"* through them (Ro.2:24). Anderson writes that

"The Jews perverted agency into a monopoly of Divine favour. That temple which was to have been a 'house of prayer for all nations' they treated as though it were not God's house, but their own, and ended by degrading it till it became at last 'a den of thieves.'" [11]

Not only did the Jews fail in their commission to be the Ministers of God they also rebelled against God *"til there was no remedy"*:

"They mocked the messengers of God, and despised His words, and misused His prophets, until the wrath of the Lord arose against His people, till there was no remedy" (2 Chor.36:16).

16

Jerusalem was then destroyed by invading forces, and the Jews who escaped death were carried away captive to Babylon. During this time the prophets began to foretell of a time when the children of Israel would be brought back to their land and the Lord would pour out His spirit upon the nation for empowerment:

"And it shall come to pass afterward, that I will pour out my spirit upon all flesh; and your sons and your daughters shall prophesy, your old men shall dream dreams, your young men shall see visions: And also upon the servants and upon the hand-maids in those days will I pour out my spirit" (Joel 2:28-29).

This also refers to the time when the "Redeemer" would come to Israel and the Lord would put His "words" into the mouths of the Israelites:

"And the Redeemer shall come to Zion, and unto them that turn from transgression in Jacob, saith the LORD. As for me, this is my covenant with them, saith the LORD; My spirit that is upon thee, and my words which I have put in thy mouth, shall not depart out of thy mouth, nor out of the mouth of thy seed, nor out of the mouth of thy seed's seed, saith the LORD, from henceforth and for ever" (Isa.59:20-21).

The "word of God" and the "pouring out of the Spirit" distinguished the stewardship which followed the "Dispensation of the Law."

III. The Dispensation of the Word and the Spirit

"The Law was added because of transgressions, until the seed should come to whom the promise was made...which is Jesus Christ" (Gal.3:16,19).

The dispensation of the Law was to last only until the beginning of the ministry of the Lord Jesus:

"the law was added...until the seed should come...which is Jesus Christ."

Anderson wrote that the ministry of the Lord Jesus represented the beginning of a new dispensation:

"Every one recognises that the advent of Christ marked a signal 'change of dispensation,' as it is termed: that is, a change in God's dealing with man." [12]

Although the Law remained an integral part of the lives of the Jews a new stewardship was put in place. Anderson wrote that the Mosaic economy was a state of tutelage which ended with the coming of Christ:

"In the Mosaic economy, religion and morality had prominence...These were like guides which were followed in the darkness till the goal was reached to which they led. The Mosaic economy was a state of tutelage which ended with the coming of Christ." [13]

The Word

John the Baptist was sent as a forerunner of Jesus to preach that the gospel that the "kingdom of heaven is at hand":

"In those days came John the Baptist, preaching in the wilderness of Judaea, And saying, Repent ye: for the kingdom of heaven is at hand" (Mt.3:1-2).

Anderson says the following about the gospel which John preached:

"The same testimony was afterwards taken up by the Lord Himself, and in due course entrusted to His Apostles. The popular belief that it was meant to herald what we call the 'Christian dispensation' is utterly mistaken. 'The kingdom of the heavens' (for such is the right rendering of the Greek words) occurs three-and-thirty times in Matthew, and nowhere else in the New Testament.

What are we to understand by the phrase? It cannot mean that God would soon begin to rule the heavens! And the only possible alternative is that the time was near when He would assume the government of earth. " [14]

After announcing that the *"kingdom of heaven is at hand"* the Lord Jesus began to declare, in the Sermon of the Mount (Mt.5-7), some of the principles which will be in force when the kingdom will be set up on earth. Anderson says:

"Our Lord was there unfolding the principles of the promised kingdom, and giving precepts for the guidance of those who were awaiting its establishment...And what a meaning the prayer for daily bread had for those who were enjoined to carry neither purse nor scrip, but to trust their heavenly Father to feed them as He feeds the birds; for, like the birds, they had 'neither storehouse nor barn.' Principles are unchanging, but the definite precepts recorded in such passages as Matt. v. 39-42 and vi. 25-34 were framed with reference to the circumstances of the time, and to the special testimony which the kingdom disciple was to maintain. " [15]

The Spirit

According to Anderson the Lord Jesus' testimony at that time was of a "twofold" nature:

"The testimony had a twofold accompaniment. 'The Sermon on the Mount' is recorded as embodying the great truths and principles which were associated with the Kingdom Gospel; and the attendant miracles gave proof that all was Divine. " [16]

The Lord Jesus' testimony was the preaching of the "gospel of the kingdom" and included the miracles which testified that all was of God. He was given the power to do miracles at the time when He was anointed with the Holy Spirit:

"God anointed Jesus of Nazareth with the Holy Spirit and power, and how he went around doing good and healing all who were under the power of the devil, because God was with him" (Acts 10:38; NIV).

Miracles are described as being gifts of the Spirit:

"Now concerning spiritual gifts, brethren, I would not have you ignorant...now there are diversities of gifts, but the same Spirit...for to one is given by the Spirit the word of wisdom...to another the gifts of healing by the same Spirit; to another the working of miracles" (1 Cor.12:1,4,8-10).

Next we see that the Lord Jesus sent His Apostles to preach the "gospel of the kingdom" and the healing and miracles which they performed gave proof that their ministry was of God:

"These twelve Jesus sent forth, and commanded them, saying, Go not into the way of the Gentiles, and into any city of the Samaritans enter not; But go, rather, to the lost sheep of the house of Israel. And as you go, preach, saying, The Kingdom of Heaven is at hand. Heal the sick, cleanse the lepers, raise the dead, cast out demons..." (Mt.10:5-8).

Later, He sent out "seventy" of His disciples to preach the same gospel and these disciples were also empowered by the Spirit of God to perform miracles:

"Heal the sick that are there, and say unto them, The Kingdom of God is come near unto you" (Lk.10:9).

Anderson states that at that time the kingdom was not an accomplished fact:

"When the Lord began to preach, the kingdom was not presented as a fact accomplished in His advent, but as a hope the realization of which, though at the very door, was still to be fulfilled. He took up the Baptist's testimony, 'The kingdom of heaven is at hand.' His ministry was a preparation for the kingdom, leading up to the time when in fulfillment of the prophetic Scriptures

He should publicly declare Himself as the Son of David, the King of Israel, and claim the homage of the nation." [17]

However, there were some Jews who began to deny that the miracles which He did were a result of God's empowerment:

"And He was casting out a demon, and it was mute; when the demon had gone out, the mute man spoke; and the crowds were amazed. But some of them said, 'He casts out demons by Beelzebul, the ruler of the demons' " (Lk.11:14-15; NASB).

After seeing the Lord Jesus perform one of his many miracles the leaders of Israel decided that He must die:

"Then saith he to the man, Stretch forth thine hand. And he stretched it forth; and it was restored whole, like as the other. Then the Pharisees went out, and held a council against him, how they might destroy him" (Mt.12:13-14).

Anderson says that after this "His teaching became veiled in parables":

"From that hour His ministry entered upon a new phase. The miracles continued, for He could not meet with suffering and refuse to relieve it; but those whom thus He blessed were charged 'that they should not make Him known' (Matthew xii. 16). The Gospel of the Kingdom ceased; His teaching became veiled in parables, and the disciples were forbidden any longer to testify to His Messiahship (Matthew xvi. 20)." [18]

Next, Anderson says that it was not until the Lord Jesus' last visit to Jerusalem when He proclaimed His Messiahship:

"No student of the Gospel narrative can fail to see that the Lord's last visit to Jerusalem was not only in fact, but in the purpose of it, the crisis of His ministry, the goal towards which it had been directed. After the first tokens had been given that the nation would reject His Messianic claims, He had shunned all public recognition of them. But now the twofold testimony of His words and His works had been fully rendered, and His entry into the

Holy City was to proclaim His Messiahship and to receive His doom." [19]

Here we see the Lord Jesus' entry into Jerusalem and He accepted the acclamations of his disciples that He is the promised Messiah or King:

"On the next day much people that were come to the feast, when they heard that Jesus was coming to Jerusalem, Took branches of palm trees, and went forth to meet him, and cried, Hosanna: Blessed is the King of Israel that cometh in the name of the Lord" (Jn.12:12-13).

Not long after this the Jewish authorities finalized their plans for His death (Mt.26:3-4) and arrested Him (Mt.26:50). Next they took Him before the high priest and there it was decreed that He was guilty of death (Mk.14:64). Then He was delivered to Pilate, and Pilate delivered Him to be crucified:

"Then delivered he him therefore unto them to be crucified. And they took Jesus, and led him away. And he bearing his cross went forth into a place called the place of a skull, which is called in the Hebrew Golgotha: Where they crucified him, and two other with him, on either side one, and Jesus in the midst. And Pilate wrote a title, and put it on the cross. And the writing was JESUS OF NAZARETH THE KING OF THE JEWS" (Jn.19:16-19).

Sir Robert says that the Lord Jesus' death upon the Cross was the world's crisis:

"He had laid aside His glory, and come down into the scene. At His own door He had stood and knocked, but only to find it shut in His face. Turning thence, He had wandered an outcast into the world which His power had made, but He wandered there unknown. 'His own received Him not'; 'the world knew Him not.' As He had laid aside His glory, He now restrained His power, and yielded Himself to their guilty will. In return for pity He earned but scorn. Sowing kindnesses and benefits with a lavish hand He reaped but cruelty and outrage. Manifesting grace He

was given up to impious law without show of mercy or pretence of justice. Unfolding the boundless love of the mighty heart of God He gained no response but bitterest hate from the hearts of men. THE SON OF GOD HAS DIED AT THE HANDS OF MEN! This astounding fact is the moral centre of all things. A bygone eternity knew no other future: an eternity to come shall know no other past. That death was this world's crisis." [20]

Anderson writes that even though the Jews had been responsible for the Lord Jesus' crucifixion Divine mercy held back the judgment which they deserved:

"The Jews had crucified the Messiah. But now, when vengeance swift and terrible might have been expected to fall upon that guilty people, Divine mercy held back the judgment and called them once again to repentance. The testimony was full and clear, and it was confirmed by a signal display of miraculous power." [21]

Due to the Lord Jesus' intercessory prayer upon the cross Divine forgiveness was secured for Israel:

"Father, forgive them; for they know not what they do"(Lk.23: 34).

After the Lord Jesus was crucified His body was placed in a tomb and then in a short time later He was resurrected from the dead. He was then seen by many in His resurrected body. These events are summed up in the following way:

"Christ died for our sins according to the Scriptures, that he was buried, that he was raised on the third day according to the Scriptures, and that he appeared to Peter, and then to the Twelve. After that, he appeared to more than five hundred of the brothers at the same time, most of whom are still living, though some have fallen asleep. Then he appeared to James, then to all the apostles" (1 Cor.15:1-7).

After His resurrection the Lord Jesus remained with His disciples for forty days before He ascended into heaven. While with them He told them to remain in Jerusalem where they would receive power after the Holy Spirit was come upon them (Acts 1:4-8). On the day of Pentecost this power came upon those gathered in His name when they began to speak in other languages, languages of which they had no knowledge (Acts 2:4-11). Peter said that what was happening then was a fulfillment of prophecy:

"But this is that which was spoken by the prophet Joel; And it shall come to pass in the last days, saith God, I will pour out of my Spirit upon all flesh: and your sons and your daughters shall prophesy, and your young men shall see visions, and your old men shall dream dreams: And on my servants and on my handmaidens I will pour out in those days of my Spirit; and they shall prophesy" (Acts 2:16-18).

Later Peter preached the facts of the resurrection of the Lord Jesus and then summed up his message when he said:

"Therefore let all the house of Israel know assuredly, that God hath made the same Jesus, whom ye have crucified, both Lord and Christ" (Acts 2:36).

Then a short time later the nation of Israel was told to repent and if she did then the Lord Jesus would be sent back to them. Anderson says that a national repentance would have resulted in the return of Christ:

"Here are the Apostle Peter's words to the Jerusalem Jews who had crucified the Messiah: 'Repent ye therefore, and turn again, that your sins may be blotted out, that so there may come seasons of refreshing from the presence of the Lord; and that He may send the Christ who hath been appointed for you even Jesus whom the heaven must receive until the times of restoration of all things, where of God spake by the mouth of His holy prophets which have been since the world began.' (Acts iii. 19-21 R.V.). 'Seasons of refreshing,' 'the times of restoration of all things,' or in other words, the times when everything shall be put right on this earth of ours, have a large place in all Hebrew prophecy from Moses to Malachi. And the Apostle proclaimed that a na-

tional repentance would bring them these times of gladness and blessing, by the return of the Messiah." [22]

Instead of repenting, the leaders of Israel imprisoned the Apostles:

"And laid their hands on the apostles, and put them in the common prison" (Acts 5:18).

The crisis of the "Dispensation of the Word and Spirit" came when Spirit-filled Stephen was brought before the Great Council of Israel. There he saw the Lord Jesus standing at the right hand of the Father:

"But he, being full of the Holy Spirit, looked up stedfastly into heaven, and saw the glory of God, and Jesus standing on the right hand of God, And said, Behold, I see the heavens opened, and the Son of man standing on the right hand of God" (Acts 7:55-56).

Anderson explains the significance of the Lord Jesus "standing" on the right hand of God:

"In Hebrews 10:11-13, the fact of His being 'seated' is emphasised as of the highest doctrinal importance but here He is seen 'standing.' May we not read this in the light of the great Pentecostal proclamation of Acts 3:19,20? The Lord is here seen in an attitude of expectancy. But the murder of Stephen was the crisis of the nation's destiny. The Lord's prayer upon the Cross had secured forgiveness for His own murderers. But the death of Stephen was, in effect, a repetition of that greatest of all human sins; and his murder was more definitely the act of the Jewish nation than even the crucifixion itself. Their Roman Governors had no share in it. It was the result of a judicial decision on the part of the great council of the nation. The proto-martyr was thus the messenger sent after the King to say, 'We will not have this man to reign over us.' And the Divine answer was to call out and commission the Apostle of the Gentiles. And the Lord Jesus, till then 'standing on the right hand of God,' waiting to fulfil the Pentecostal promise, now 'sat down on the right hand of God; from

*henceforth expecting till His enemies be made His footstool '
(Hebrews 10:12,13)." [23]*

The leaders would not believe Stephen's words and they resisted the Holy Spirit, as witnessed by his words to them:

*"You stiff-necked people, with uncircumcised hearts and ears!
You are just like your fathers: You always resist the Holy Spirit!"*
(Acts 7:51; NIV).

Throughout the ages God had remained on good terms with
mankind. However, due to the crucifixion of Christ and the murder of Stephen all this changed. Anderson writes:

*"The Jew has thus lost the position of religious privilege un-
der the covenant. Every covenant has been broken, every promise
forfeited. Man's probation has closed: he is shut up to wrath, and
there is no appeal and no escape. The whole world has become
guilty before God (Rom. iii. 19). Nothing remains but the day of
judgment. But this was made the occasion for 'the revelation of a
mystery which was kept secret since the world began' (Rom. xvi.
25)-- 'the great 'mystery' of Grace in the Gospel." [24]*

Standing by and consenting unto Stephen's death was Saul
(Paul), the leader of the rebellion against Christ, who was chosen
by God to usher in a new dispensation, the Dispensation of the
Grace of God.

*"And cast him (Stephen) out of the city, and stoned him: and
the witnesses laid down their clothes at a young man's feet, whose
name was Saul...And Saul was consenting unto his death"* (Acts
7:58; 8:1).

IV. The Dispensation of the Gospel of Grace

When it became evident that the nation of Israel would not be
a blessing to the Gentiles according to her stewardship the nation

was dismissed as His agent upon the earth. Sir Robert explains this change of dispensation or stewardship, writing that

"Thus deprived of their stewardship, they are relegated to the position of other men. And the purpose and effect of their fall are stated in the words, 'God hath concluded them all in unbelief that He might have mercy upon all' (Romans xi. 32). Thus it was that the way was opened up for the revelation of the great 'mystery' truth of grace enthroned." [25]

The Lord would not allow Israel's unbelief to interfere with His plan to have the Gentiles hear the "gospel of Christ" so Paul was chosen to be His new agent upon the earth.

Paul was fanatic in his opposition to the disciples of Christ (Acts 26:9-11). Shortly after consenting to the death of Stephen he journeyed and came near unto Damascus when suddenly there shone round about him a light from heaven and he fell to earth (Acts 9:3-4). There the Lord Jesus told him:

"Rise, and stand upon thy feet; for I have appeared unto thee for this purpose...to make thee a minister and a wit- ness...delivering thee from the people, and from the Gentiles, unto whom now I send thee...to open their eyes...that they may receive forgiveness of sins and inheritance among them who are sancti- fied by faith that is in me" (Acts 26:16-18).

Anderson writes that Paul now received the call to his great ministry:

"The Apostle (Peter) proclaimed that a national repentance would bring them these times of gladness and blessing, by the re- turn of the Messiah...The nation having proved impenitent, God deferred the realization of these promises. Like their fathers in the days of Moses and of David, 'they entered not in because of unbelief.' The 'Apostle to the Gentiles' received the call to his great ministry." [26]

The fulfillment of the promises made to Israel according to prophecy has been put on hold and a new dispensation that was not revealed in the Old Testament was ushered in by the Apostle Paul. He described his dispensational responsibilities in the following way:

"Unto me, who am less than the least of all saints, was this grace given, to preach unto the Gentiles the unsearchable riches of Christ; and to make all men see what is the dispensation of the mystery which for ages hath been hid in God who created all things" (Eph.3:8-9; ASV).

The truths which Paul preached in his gospel would be seached for in vain in the Old Testament so he describes them as being the "unsearchable riches of Christ." Since what he preached was not revealed he describes the present dispensation as the "dispensation of the mystery" and that this has been hidden in God.

The Meaning of the Term "Dispensation of Grace"

The evidence from the Scriptures makes it abundantly clear that the "dispensation of grace" is in regard to the duty of preaching the "gospel of grace." Let us look at the following three verses from the pen of Paul:

"Whereof I am made a minister, according to the dispensation of God which is given to me for you, to fulfil the word of God" (Col.1:25).

"...a dispensation of the gospel is committed unto me" (1 Cor. 9:17).

"If ye have heard of the dispensation of the grace of God which is given me toward you..." (Eph.3:2).

The "dispensation" that was committed to Paul was in regard to a "ministry," a "gospel," and "God's grace." The following

words of Paul refer to these three things and therefore demonstrate that his dispensational responsibility was to preach the gospel of grace:

*"But none of these things move me, neither count I my life
dear unto myself, so that I might finish my course with joy, and
the ministry, which I have received of the Lord Jesus, to testify the
gospel of the grace of God"* (Acts 20: 24).

The stewardship responsibility which is in effect at the present
time is to preach the gospel of grace. Sir Robert says that this
gospel was not previously preached by the other Apostles:

*" 'My Gospel.' The words, three times repeated by St. Paul,
are no mere conventional expression. They are explained in several of his Epistles, and with peculiar definiteness in his letter to
the Galatians. He there declares in explicit and emphatic terms
that the gospel which he preached among the Gentiles was the
subject of a special revelation peculiar to himself. Not only was
he not taught it by those who were apostles before him, but he it
was who, by Divine command, communicated it to 'the twelve';
and this was not until his second visit to Jerusalem, seventeen
years after his conversion. It is certain, therefore, that his testimony was essentially distinct in character and scope from anything we shall find in the ministry of the other apostles, recorded
in the Acts."* [27]

William R. Newell wrote that the Apostles who preceded Paul
were not the first to teach the "great body of doctrine for this
age":

*"The twelve Apostles (Matthias by Divine appointment taking
the place of Judas) were to be the 'witnesses' (Acts 1:22) of
Christ's resurrection--that is, of the fact of it. They were not to
unfold fully the doctrine of it, as Paul was...But unto none of these
twelve Apostles did God reveal 'the great body of doctrine for this
age'...The great doctrines that Paul reveals may be outlined as
follows...The fact and the Scripturalness of righteousness on the*

free gift principle--that is, of Divine righteousness, separate from all man's doings, conferred upon man as a free gift from God." [28]

After reading this Bible tract Lewis Sperry Chafer, the founding President of Dallas Theological Seminary, said:

"This is a great tract, a clear treatise on the truth of God for this age. The author was one of America's greatest Bible expositors. It glorifies the Savior as the author desired it to do. It should be distributed by hundreds of thousands." [29]

The second President of Dallas Theological Seminary, John F. Walvoord, wrote that *"The gospel of Grace was given to Paul as a 'new' revelation."* [30]

Charles Ryrie, Professor Emeritus at Dallas Theological Seminary for many years, wrote the following:

"The apostle Paul was principally, though not exclusively, the agent of the revelation of the grace of God for this dispensation. Christ Himself brought the grace of God to mankind in His incarnation (Titus 2:11), but Paul was the one who expounded it." [31]

The Gospel of Grace

Sir Robert explains the events leading up to the revelation of the "gospel of grace" and then makes comments on the gospel itself:

"When God took up the Hebrews as His favoured people and brought them into special relationship with Himself, covenant superseded Grace as the characteristic of the Jewish dispensation. But when that people became the betrayers and murderers of Christ, when the Cross stood between an outraged God and a guilty and doomed world, then the only possible alternatives were grace and judgment. God must either deal with men according to their deserts, or else, in infinite mercy and love, pardon and bless them in spite of all. And this, and nothing less than this, is 'the Gospel of the grace of God.' 'God so loved the world that He gave

30

His only-begotten Son, that whosoever believeth in Him should not perish, but have everlasting life. For God sent not His Son into the world to condemn the world, but that the world through Him might be saved.' 'By grace are ye saved, through faith, and that (salvation) not of yourselves, it is the gift of God; not of works, lest any one should boast.' 'The wages of sin is death' (that is what men have earned), 'but the gift of God is eternal life in Christ Jesus our Lord.' A gift may be deserved, but these words are the climax of an argument in which it is emphatically called 'the gift by grace.' " [32]

Sir Robert says that in the present dispensation "grace reigns":

"God's attitude toward men is grace. 'GRACE REIGNS.' It is not that there is grace for the penitent or the elect, but that grace is the principle on which Christ now sits upon the throne of God. 'Upon His head are many crowns, but His pierced hand now holds the only scepter,' for the Father has given Him the kingdom; all power is His in heaven and on earth. 'The Father judgeth no man, but hath committed all judgment to the Son' (John v. 22; Compare iii. 17 and xii. 47); but His mission to earth was not to judge, but only to save. And He who is thus the only Judge is now exalted to be a Savior, and the throne on which He sits is a throne of grace. Grace is reigning, through righteousness, unto eternal life (Romans v. 21). The light of this glorious gospel now shines unhindered upon earth. Blind eyes may shut it out, but they cannot quench or lessen it. Impenitent hearts may heap up wrath against the day of wrath, but they cannot darken this day of mercy or mar the glory of the reign of grace." [33]

The End of the Dispensation of the Gospel of Grace

Before the present "dispensation of grace" began those belonging to the nation of Israel were described as being "above" all other people:

"For thou art an holy people unto the LORD thy God: the LORD thy God hath chosen thee to be a special people unto him-

self, above all people that are upon the face of the earth" (Deut.7:6).

However, during the present stewardship all distinction between the Jews and the rest of mankind has been done away. Anderson points out this truth:

"Thus deprived of their stewardship, they (Israel) are relegated to the position of other men...Language could not be more explicit 'All the world is brought under the judgment of God' (Romans iii. 19); 'There is no difference between the Jew and the Greek' (Romans x. 12)." [34]

After the present dispensation runs its course the children of Israel will regain their position as a *"special people unto himself, above all people that are upon the face of the earth."* Anderson writes that the Scriptures reveal that Israel will be restored to her previous favored position:

"The very same Scripture which teaches this declares with equal clearness and emphasis that 'the gifts and calling of God are without repentance'; that 'God has not cast away His people'; that 'they are beloved for the fathers' sakes,' and that they are yet to be restored to the favoured position which they have now lost through unbelief." [35]

Sir Robert states that some crisis must intervene before Israel will be restored to the favored position that she once enjoyed:

"Now in the same sense in which we aver that God cannot lie, we may aver that He cannot act upon incompatible principles at the same time. Therefore, so long as the proclamation is in force that 'there is no difference between the Jew and the Gentile,' God cannot make a difference by giving the Jew a position of peculiar privilege and favour. It follows, therefore, that the present dispensation cannot merge gradually in the dispensation which is to follow it. The change must be marked by a crisis." [36]

Here Sir Robert explains what that "crisis" will be:

"I refer to the neglected truth of the Coming of the Lord Jesus Christ to take His people home from earth to heaven. 'For the Lord Himself shall descend from heaven with a shout, with the voice of the archangel, and with the trump of God; and the dead in Christ shall rise first; then we which are alive and remain, shall be caught up together with them in the clouds, to meet the Lord in the air; and so shall we ever be with the Lord' (1 Thess.4:16,17)." [37]

Anderson explains that after this event the nation of Israel will once again be the center of Divine action toward mankind:

"With this event this special 'day of grace' will cease, and God will again revert to 'the covenants' and 'the promises,' and that people to whom the covenants and promises belong will once more become the center of Divine action toward mankind." [38]

Resumption of The Dispensation of the Word and the Spirit

During the "dispensation of grace" the things pertaining to national Israel were put on hold but the prophecies concerning that nation will begin to have their fulfillment after the present dispensation comes to a close. Here Anderson explains that after the present dispensation in which we are living comes to an end then the nation of Israel will have to endure the "great tribulation":

"This present age will end with that Coming of Christ which is revealed in the Epistles. And not until after that great crisis will the apocalyptic visions receive their fulfilment. The Abrahamic seed will then have been restored to their normal position as the Covenant people of God; even though, as foretold by the Lord Himself in Matthew 24, they will still have to endure the terrible ordeal of 'the great tribulation' of Old Testament prophecy." [39]

Sir Robert next speaks of the resumption of the dispensation which was broken off during the Acts period:

" 'God has not cast away His people;' and when the present dispensation closes, and the great purpose has been satisfied for which it was ordained, the dropped threads of prophecy and promise will again be taken up, and the dispensation historically broken off in the Acts of the Apostles, when Jerusalem was the appointed center for God's people on earth, will be resumed. Judah shall again become a nation, Jerusalem shall be restored, and that temple shall be built in which the "abomination of desolation" is to stand." [40]*

Let us look at verses from the twenty-fourth chapter of Matthew which speak of the events leading up to the "abomination of desolation" and the "great tribulation":

"And this gospel of the kingdom shall be preached in all the world for a witness unto all nations; and then shall the end come. When ye therefore shall see the abomination of desolation, spoken of by Daniel the prophet, stand in the holy place, (whoso readeth, let him understand:) Then let them which be in Judaea flee into the mountains" (Mt.24:14-16).

Here we see that once again the "*gospel of the kingdom shall be preached*" (Mt. 24:14), showing that the previous stewardship responsibility during the "dispensation of the Word and Spirit" to preach that gospel will be resumed after the "dispensation of grace" comes to an end.

Anderson distinguishes between the gospel which we are to preach at the present time from the "gospel of the kingdom":

"We know, however, that before His Coming to His earthly people 'the gospel of the kingdom will be preached in the whole world for a testimony to all the nations' - not the gospel of this age of grace, but the gospel of the kingdom." [41]

Not long after the "abomination of desolation" stands in the Holy Place as recorded at Matthew 24:15 the nation of Israel will have to endure the "great tribulation":

"But pray ye that your flight be not in the winter, neither on the sabbath day: For then shall be great tribulation, such as was not since the beginning of the world to this time, no, nor ever shall be. And except those days should be shortened, there should no flesh be saved: but for the elect's sake those days shall be shortened...Immediately after the tribulation of those days shall the sun be darkened, and the moon shall not give her light, and the stars shall fall from heaven, and the powers of the heavens shall be shaken" (Mt.24:20-22,29).

Sir Robert says that the description of the signs in the sky which follow the great tribulation are also described at Revelation 6:12-14:

"According to the twenty-fourth chapter of Matthew, the tribulation is to be followed immediately by the signs and portents which the old prophets have declared will herald 'the great and terrible day of the Lord.' So in the Apocalypse the martyrs of the tribulation are seen in the fifth seal (Rev. vi. 9), and in the sixth, the advent of the great day of wrath is proclaimed, the precise events being named which the Lord had spoken of on the Mount of Olives, and Joel and Isaiah had foretold long centuries before." [42]

First there will be a "great tribulation" that is in regard to Israel only, and then this tribulation will be followed by signs in the heavenly sphere and then following those signs the people of the earth will be in fear of things which they are expecting to be coming to the earth:

"And there shall be signs in the sun, and in the moon, and in the stars; and upon the earth distress of nations, with perplexity; the sea and the waves roaring; Men's hearts failing them for fear, and for looking after those things which are coming on the earth: for the powers of heaven shall be shaken" (Lk.21:25-26).

These events are also described at Revelation 6:12-17, where those who are in fear say:

"Hide us from the face of him that sitteth on the throne, and from the wrath of the Lamb: For the great day of his wrath is come; and who shall be able to stand?" (Rev.24:16-17).

Sometimes after this the following prophecies revealed by John will take place:

"And I stood upon the sand of the sea, and saw a beast rise up out of the sea, having seven heads and ten horns, and upon his horns ten crowns, and upon his heads the name of blasphemy...And it was given unto him to make war with the saints, and to overcome them: and power was given him over all kindreds, and tongues, and nations. And all that dwell upon the earth shall worship him, whose names are not written in the book of life of the Lamb slain from the foundation of the world" (Rev.13:1,7-8).

This will be the time when signs and wonders will be employed to deceive mankind:

"And he exerciseth all the power of the first beast before him, and causeth the earth and them which dwell therein to worship the first beast, whose deadly wound was healed. And he doeth great wonders, so that he maketh fire come down from heaven on the earth in the sight of men, And deceiveth them that dwell on the earth by the means of those miracles which he had power to do in the sight of the beast" (Rev.13:12-14).

Commenting on these verses Anderson says:

"The signs and wonders of Satanic power shall still command the homage of mankind, while the thunders of a heaven no longer silent will break forth upon the apostate race. Then will be the time of 'the seven last plagues,' wherein 'is filled up the wrath of God,' — the time when 'the vials of the wrath of God' shall be poured out upon the earth (Rev.xv. 1; xvi. 1). And if in this day of grace the heights and depths of God's longsuffering mercy transcend all human thoughts, His WRATH will be no less Divine. 'The day of vengeance of our God,' 'the great and the terrible

day of the Lord,' — such are the names divinely given to describe that time of unexampled horror." [43]

The Lord Jesus will then arrive on the scene to bring to a close this time of unexampled horror and to take vengeance on all who know not God:

"And I saw heaven opened, and behold a white horse; and he that sat upon him was called Faithful and True, and in righteousness he doth judge and make war...And out of his mouth goeth a sharp sword, that with it he should smite the nations: and he shall rule them with a rod of iron: and he treadeth the winepress of the fierceness and wrath of Almighty God. And he hath on his vesture and on his thigh a name written, KING OF KINGS, AND LORD OF LORDS" (Rev.19:11,15-16).

In regard to this time Anderson writes that

"Our Jehovah-God will come with all His holy ones; the Lord Jesus will be revealed in flaming fire, taking vengeance (II Thess. i. 7,8)." [44]

Here are the verses to which he makes reference:

"...when the Lord Jesus shall be revealed from heaven with his mighty angels, In flaming fire taking vengeance on them that know not God, and that obey not the gospel of our Lord Jesus Christ: Who shall be punished with everlasting destruction from the presence of the Lord, and from the glory of his power" (2 Thess.1:7-9).

It will be at this time when He will set up the kingdom on earth:

"And then shall they see the Son of man coming in a cloud with power and great glory...when ye see these things come to pass, know ye that the kingdom of God is nigh at hand" (Lk.21:27,31).

"When the Son of man shall come in his glory, and all the holy angels with him, then shall he sit upon the throne of his glory" (Mt.25:31).

VI. The Dispensation of the Righteous Rule of the King

Anderson describes the dispensation when the Lord Jesus shall rule as King as being the time when the kingdom will be established *"in righteousness and peace"*:

"The day would surely come…when *evil should be rooted out, and the kingdom established in righteousness and peace (Matt. xiii. 41-43)."* [45]

Here are the verses to which he makes reference:

"The Son of man shall send forth his angels, and they shall gather out of his kingdom all things that offend, and them which do iniquity; And shall cast them into a furnace of fire: there shall be wailing and gnashing of teeth. Then shall the righteous shine forth as the sun in the kingdom of their Father" (Mt.13:41-43).

Sir Robert says that at that time heaven shall rule upon the earth:

"Earth's history, as unfolded in the Scriptures, reaches on to a Sabbatic age of blessedness and peace; an age when heaven shall rule upon the earth, when, 'the Lord shall rejoice in all His works,' and prove Himself to be the God of every creature He has made." [46]

The dispensation under discussion is in regard to the "kingdom of heaven," the same kingdom which the Lord Jesus heralded as being at hand at the beginning of His ministry.

Anderson writes that during the "dispensation of the Righteous Rule of the King" that "sorrow and discord should give place to gladness and peace":

"But type and promise and prophecy testified with united voice that the advent of Messiah should be the dawn of a brighter day, when 'the heavens should rule,' when all wrong should be redressed, and sorrow and discord should give place to gladness and peace. The angelic host who heralded His birth confirmed the testimony, and seemed to point to its near fulfilment." [47]

But as we have seen, the nation of Israel refused to repent and turn to the Lord and the Lord Jesus was not sent back at that time. During the present "dispensation of grace" the Lord Jesus remains in heaven but during the "dispensation of the Righteous Rule of the King" He will be present on the earth.

Sir Robert acknowledges these truths:

"This is the age of His absence, but the coming age shall be characterized by His presence. Not an isolated event, albeit Scripture tells us that a series of manifestations of Christ will make its course, but a new attitude toward men — immediate divine action both in blessing and in judgment. For while the covert atheism of these days of ours scoffs at the thought that the prayer which He Himself has put into our lips could ever be fulfilled, His believing people know that His kingdom is certainly coming, and that His will shall be done on earth." [48]

The following Old Testament words foretell of this kingdom:

"The earth shall be full of the knowledge of the LORD, as the waters cover the sea. And in that day there shall be a root of Jesse, which shall stand for an ensign of the people; to it shall the Gentiles seek: and his rest shall be glorious" (Isa.11:9-10).

The prophet Zechariah describes this time in the following way:

"And the LORD shall be king over all the earth: in that day shall there be one LORD, and his name one...And it shall come to pass, that every one that is left of all the nations which came against Jerusalem shall even go up from year to year to worship

the King, the LORD of hosts, and to keep the feast of tabernacles"
(Zech.14:9,16).

Now let us look at the following verses which describe the
end of the earthly kingdom:

*"And when the thousand years are expired, Satan shall be
loosed out of his prison, And shall go out to deceive the nations
which are in the four quarters of the earth, Gog, and Magog, to
gather them together to battle: the number of whom is as the sand
of the sea. And they went up on the breadth of the earth, and
compassed the camp of the saints about, and the beloved city: and
fire came down from God out of heaven, and devoured them. And
the devil that deceived them was cast into the lake of fire and
brimstone, where the beast and the false prophet are, and shall be
tormented day and night for ever and ever"* (Rev.20:7-10).

In his commentary on these verses Anderson writes:

*"After the millennial reign, Satan is loosed, and once more
deceives the nations. Satan is cast into the lake of fire."* [49]

After this the Lord Jesus will deliver up the kingdom to God:

*"Then cometh the end, when he shall have delivered up the
kingdom to God, even the Father; when he shall have put down
all rule and all authority and power. For he must reign, till he
hath put all enemies under his feet...And when all things shall be
subdued unto him, then shall the Son also himself be subject unto
him that put all things under him, that God may be all in all"* (1
Cor.15:24,25,28).

VII. The Dispensation of the Fullness of Times

*"That in the dispensation of the fullness of times He might
gather together in one all things in Christ, both which are in
heaven, and which are on earth, even in Him"* (Eph.1:10).

This is when all the saved from all ages will be gathered into the Lord and into the "eternal state", where God has dwelt throughout eternity:

"For thus saith the high and lofty One that inhabiteth eternity, whose name is Holy; I dwell in the high and holy place, with Him also that is of a contrite and humble spirit" (Isa. 57:15).

Sir Robert writes that at "the end" time will have run its course:

" 'IN THE BEGINNING' the Word was alone with God; and on through the ages of ages to 'THE END', when, time having running its course, in the midst of His creation, God shall be all in all: and in adoration he exclaims, 'From everlasting to ever-lasting Thou art God !'" [50]

It will not be until the created universe is destroyed that time will have run its course. Here is a description of the events which will usher in the "Dispensation of the Fullness of Times," when time will be no more:

"But the day of the Lord will come as a thief in the night; in the which the heavens shall pass away with a great noise, and the elements shall melt with fervent heat, the earth also and the works that are therein shall be burned up. Seeing then that all these things shall be dissolved, what manner of persons ought ye to be in all holy conversation and godliness, Looking for and hasting unto the coming of the day of God, wherein the heavens being on fire shall be dissolved, and the elements shall melt with fervent heat?" (2 Pet.10-11).

Sir Robert provides the following commentary on these verses:

"True it is that this earth that has been the scene of the pandemonium, shall yet be given up to fire, but not till every word of Hebrew prophecy has been fulfilled; for no word can fail that God has ever uttered. 'We according to His promise, look for new

heavens and a new earth,' but this belongs to an eternity to come." [51]

Anderson says that in the eternal state:

"Heaven will join with earth, and 'the tabernacle of God'— the dwelling place of the Almighty — shall be with men, 'and He will dwell with them, and they shall be His people, and God Himself shall be with them, and be their God.' " [52]

Sir Robert points out that the Cross was not just the world's crisis but also the crisis of the whole created universe:

"It is certain that millennial blessedness and glory will be a direct result and proof of the preciousness of the cross of Christ to God; but it is no less certain that an eternity of glory and blessedness, still to follow, will depend upon that cross as really and immediately. In our view, creation limits itself to our own race and sphere, but with God the universe is one great whole, of which the Adamic world is but a part. And as sin has disturbed the harmony of Creation in this its widest sense, God's answer and remedy are the cross of Christ and a new creation. It is not merely the kingdoms of this world that are given up to Christ, but the throne of the universe of God. And when 'the end' shall come, and God shall again assume the sceptre He will hold it in virtue of Calvary. If one could dare to speak thus of God, we might say that His moral right to make all things new depends on that blood. And the word is 'I make ALL THINGS new.' The promise is not of a new earth only, but of new heavens too. And why 'new heavens,' if sin and the cross concern only earth? 'It is finished' was the cry that rose amid the agonies of Calvary: 'Behold I make all things new' is the response from the glory. The 'It is finished' of the cross, shall still vibrate until it is lost in the 'It is done' of the throne. (Rev. xxi. 5,6.)." [53]

Dispensational Survey: Conclusion

Before the "Dispensation of National Service" was assigned to Abraham and his descendants the Lord saw what was in man and here is His judgment:

"And God saw that the wickedness of man was great in the earth, and that every imagination of the thoughts of his heart was only evil continually" (Gen.6:5).

Sir Robert writes that even though God knew what was in man from the start He *"decreed that the creature should prove it to himself"*:

"At the very outset, His judgments of the matter were declared in no uncertain terms (Gen. vi. 1-5). But, in His infinite wisdom, He decreed that the creature should prove it himself. Now, He has done so." [54]

The creature has indeed proved it to himself. The different dispensations given by the Lord to man and man's subsequent failure under each dispensation is proof to man that he is a failed and miserable creature. Anderson points out that from the beginning of time man has proven himself to be lawless:

"The creature claimed his liberty, and turned prodigal. God allowed him a long probation to prove what that liberty would lead to, and the result was only evil. Tried by every possible test, man has proved himself to be utterly unrighteous. Left to the light of nature, he turned from it, and proved himself lawless. When the commandment came, he turned against it, and proved himself a transgressor." [55]

Anderson also says that Israel's failure under the stewardships which were assigned to her is "conclusive proof that Adam's race is evil":

"And the history of Israel, remember, is the history of human nature tried in the most favourable circumstances. Abraham was of our own flesh and blood. If he differed from other men, it was only that, as judged by men, he was a splendid specimen of the

race...Abraham's family, therefore, was the little Eden vineyard reclaimed from nature's wildness, and tended and nourished with the utmost care and wisdom. If then, even here, no fitting fruit was yielded, the entire stock may fairly be condemned. If the Jew is shown to have utterly failed, it is the crowning and conclusive proof that Adam's race is evil." [56]

Sir Robert goes on to say that man has no one other than himself to blame for his deplorable actions down through the ages:

"To say that man is precisely what God made him to be is sheer blasphemy. 'God made man upright.' But, it may be urged, God might have made man incapable of sin. That is, He might have created a being destitute of any independent will. Doubtless but then such a creature must needs be of a far lower order than Adam and his race. But God might in fact have prevented Adam's sin. That is, He might have created him capable of an independent will, but practically incapable of exercising it. The fact of man's apostasy is a terrible but most signal testimony to the greatness and dignity of the place from which he fell, and it ill becomes him to answer back his Maker, 'Why hast Thou made me thus?' Moreover, God has been vindicated in this respect by the life of Christ on earth; for such an one as Adam was has perfectly obeyed Him, even in the midst of suffering and sin. Nor is God's goodness at fault towards the fallen race. Man has chosen his own will, and turned from God in the pursuit of it." [57]

From a study of the different dispensations it is evident that there is nothing in man which can possibly contribute to his salvation so therefore he is entirely dependent on the mercy or grace of God if he is going to be saved.

Anderson writes that the main truths of the Christian revelation, including the "gospel of grace," were lost for centuries:

"In the interval between the Apostolic age and the era of the Patristic theologians, the main truths of the distinctively Christian revelation were lost in the Early Church and they were never

fully recovered until the Evangelical Revival of the nineteenth century." [58]

Even today these main truths of Christianity are not being preached in the majority of churches which dot the landscape. Since these truths remain effectively lost the next few chapters of this book will be devoted to a clear exposition of the "gospel of grace."

NOTES

1. Sir Robert Anderson, *The Coming Prince* (Grand Rapids: Kregel Classics, 1957), 14-15.

2. Sir Robert Anderson, *Unfulfilled Prophecy* (London: Chas. J. Thynne, 1917), 50.

3. Sir Robert Anderson, *Misunderstood Texts of the New Testament* (Grand Rapids: Kregel Publications, 1991), 13.

4. Joseph Henry Thayer, *A Greek-English Lexicon of the New Testament* [Grand Rapids: Baker Book House, 1977], 440.

5. *Ibid.*

6. Unless otherwise noted all quotations from the Scriptures are from the King James Bible.

7. Sir Robert Anderson, *The Silence of God* (Grand Rapids: Kregel Publications, 1978), 52.

8. Sir Robert Anderson, *Forgotten Truths* [Grand Rapids: Kregel Publications, 1980], 41.

9. Sir Robert Anderson, *The Bible or the Church?* (London: Pickering & Inglis, Second Edition), 63.

10. *Ibid.,* 64-65.

11. Sir Robert Anderson, *The Silence of God*, 53.

12. *Ibid.,* 177.

13. *Ibid.,* 136.

14. Sir Robert Anderson, *Misunderstood Texts of the New Testament*, 15-16.

15. Sir Robert Anderson, *The Silence of God*, 178-179.

16. Sir Robert Anderson, *The Coming Prince,* 160.

17. *Ibid.,* 125.

18. *Ibid.,* 162.

19. *Ibid.,* 125.

20. Sir Robert Anderson, *The Gospel And Its Ministry* (Grand Rapids: Kregel Publications, 1978), 13-14.

21. Sir Robert Anderson, *The Silence of God,* 78.

22. Sir Robert Anderson, *Types in Hebrews* (Grand Rapids: Kregel Publications, 1978), 87.

23. Sir Robert Anderson, *Misunderstood Texts of the New Testament,* 72-73.

24. Sir Robert Anderson, *The Bible or the Church?* 198.

25. Sir Robert Anderson, *Forgotten Truths,* 43.

26. Sir Robert Anderson, *Types in Hebrews,* 87-88.

27. Sir Robert Anderson, *The Silence of God,* 107-108.

28. William Newell, "Paul's Gospel," *Journal of the Grace Evangelical Society,* Spring 1994, Volume 7:12.

29. Editor, *Journal of the Grace Evangelical Society,* Spring 1994, Volume 7:12.

30. John F. Walvoord, "The Preincarnate Son of God", *Bibliotheca Sacra,* Oct.-Dec. 1947, Vol. 104, # 416, 422.

31. Charles Ryrie, *Dispensationalism* (Chicago: Moody Press 1995), 56.

32. Sir Robert Anderson, *The Bible or the Church?* 199-201.

33. Sir Robert Anderson, *The Coming Prince,* 144-145.

34. Sir Robert Anderson, *Forgotten Truths*, 43.

35. *Ibid.*

36. Sir Robert Anderson, *Misunderstood Texts of the New Testament*, 91.

37. Sir Robert Anderson, *Forgotten Truths*, 45.

38. Sir Robert Anderson, *The Coming Prince,* 155.

39. Sir Robert Anderson, *Misunderstood Texts of the New Testament*, 141.

40. Sir Robert Anderson, *The Coming Prince,* 169-170.

41. Sir Robert Anderson, *Misunderstood Texts of the New Testament*, 23.

42. Sir Robert Anderson, *The Coming Prince,* 174.

43. *Ibid.,* 218.

44. *Ibid.,* 289.

45. *Ibid.,* 163.

46. *Ibid.,* 218-219.

47. Sir Robert Anderson, *The Silence of God*, 13.

48. Sir Robert Anderson, *The Lord From Heaven* (Grand Rapids: Kregel Classics, 1978), 105.

49. Sir Robert Anderson, *The Coming Prince,* 178.

50. Sir Robert Anderson, *The Gospel And Its Ministry*, 152.

51. Sir Robert Anderson, *The Lord From Heaven*, 102.

52. Sir Robert Anderson, *The Coming Prince*, 219.

53. Sir Robert Anderson, *The Gospel And Its Ministry*, 149.

54. *Ibid.*, 106.

55. *Ibid.*, 105.

56. *Ibid.*, 106.

57. *Ibid.*, 105.

58. Sir Robert Anderson, *Misunderstood Texts of the New Testament*, 25.

Chapter 3

How Sinners Can Be Saved

In the first four chapters of the epistle to the *Romans* Paul unveils the only way that a sinner can be saved. In the second chapter he says that a person can obtain eternal life if he "continues" in well doing:

"But after thy hardness and impenitent heart treasurest up un-to thyself wrath against the day of wrath and revelation of the righteous judgment of God; Who will render to every man according to his deeds: To them who by patient continuance in well doing seek for glory and honour and immortality, eternal life: But unto them that are contentious, and do not obey the truth, but obey unrighteousness, indignation and wrath, Tribulation and anguish, upon every soul of man that doeth evil, of the Jew first, and also of the Gentile" (Ro.2:5-9).

Here Paul is speaking of the "judgment of God" and he says that God will render to every man according to his "deeds." The Greek word translated "deeds" means:

"The conduct of men measured by the standard of religion or righteousness." [1]

So this "judgment" is strictly in regard to a person's conduct or the things he does in his body. The standard spoken of here by which man will be judged is "law"--"the law" given to the Jew through the Mosaic Covenant and to the Gentile it is the *"works of the law which is written in the heart"* to which the conscience bears witness (Ro.2:15). To explain the Gentile's relationship to "law" Anderson writes that

"The Gentile therefore had, by virtue of his very being, the law which was formally tabulated in commandments. Having not 'the' law he was a law unto himself (Rom. ii. 14). Love to God and man, worked out in this life, is the fulfillment of the law; it is, moreover, the attainment of creature perfectness." [2]

Next, Paul makes it plain that no one is righteous before God based on keeping God's law:

"Wherefore by works of law no flesh shall be justified before him; for by law is knowledge of sin" (Ro.3:20; DBY).

Then in the next chapter Paul reveals the way that sinners are saved:

"But now a righteousness from God, apart from law, has been made known, to which the Law and the Prophets testify. This righteousness from God comes through faith in Jesus Christ to all who believe. There is no difference, for all have sinned and fall short of the glory of God, and are justified freely by his grace through the redemption that came by Christ Jesus" (Ro.3:21-24; NIV).

In his commentary on these verses Anderson says that these verses are speaking of a Divine righteousness which is not on the principle of "law":

"The Holy Spirit has come, not to reopen the question of sin and righteousness and judgment, but to convince the world that it is closed for ever. If then human righteousness - righteousness on the principle of conformity to law, the principle, namely, of man's being what he ought to be - is irrevocably set aside, there must be a revelation of righteousness which is of God, and therefore, of course, on some principle altogether different. 'But now, apart from law,' the apostle proceeds, 'righteousness which is of God is revealed, being borne witness to by the law and the prophets.' Hitherto, human righteousness has been demanded; but now, divine righteousness is revealed. We shall see presently what the principle is on which it is based; but here, we have the point set-

tled, that it is not on the principle of law. 'By deeds of law no flesh living can be justified' ; righteousness is now on a wholly different ground. The contrast is not between personal and vicarious law-keeping, but between righteousness on the principle of law-keeping, and righteousness which is entirely apart from law; between righteousness of man, worked out on earth, and righteousness of God, revealed from heaven." [3]

Paul describes some who were of Israel and were ignorant of this righteousness which is revealed from heaven:

"For they, being ignorant of God's righteousness, and seeking to establish their own righteousness, have not submitted to the righteousness of God" (Ro.10:3-4; DBY).

Paul distinguishes between a righteousness which is based on the principle of law keeping and a righteousness which is of God, a righteousness that is received by believing:

"...and that I may be found in him, not having my righteousness, which would be on the principle of law, but that which is by faith of Christ, the righteousness which is of God through faith" (Phil.3:9; DBY).

Paul also makes it plain that those who believe are no longer to be judged by law in regard to obtaining a righteous standing before God:

"For Christ is the end of law for righteousness to every one that believes" (Ro.10:4; DBY).

Paul also speaks of the believing remnant out of national Israel and says that their election is of grace and therefore "it is no more of works":

"Even so then at this present time also there is a remnant according to the election of grace. And if by grace, then is it no more of works: otherwise grace is no more grace" (Ro.11:5-6).

Sir Robert addresses these two different means of obtaining a "justification" before God which are revealed by Paul in the epistle to the Romans:

"There are two alternative principles on which alone justification is now theoretically possible. The one is by man's deserving it; the other is through God's unmerited favour. Let a man, from the cradle to the grave, be everything he ought to be, and do everything he ought to do; let him...love God with all his heart, and his neighbour as himself, walking 'purely, humbly, and beneficently while on earth,' and such an one will 'inherit eternal life.' But all such pretensions betoken moral and spiritual ignorance and degradation. All men are sinners; and being sinners they are absolutely dependent upon grace." [4]

It is the "gospel of grace" which brings the righteousness which is of God unto everyone who believes it.

Anderson says:

"The Gospel brings peace to the sinner, not because it makes light of his sin, or lowers the inexorable claims of Divine perfection, but because it tells how Christ has made it possible for an absolutely righteous and thrice holy God to pardon and save absolutely sinful and evil men." [5]

The Apostle Paul is silent in regard to a salvation that is based on "faith" plus "works" despite the fact that there are many denominations within Christianity which teach that "works" of one kind or another are required. These denominations fail to recognize that the reward comes to those who "worketh not," but believeth:

"Now to him that worketh is the reward not reckoned of grace, but of debt. But to him that worketh not, but believeth on him that justifieth the ungodly, his faith is counted for righteousness" (Ro.4:4-5).

NOTES

1. Joseph Henry Thayer, *A Greek-English Lexicon of the New Testament*, 248.

2. Sir Robert Anderson, *The Gospel And Its Ministry*, 149.

3. *Ibid.*, 108-109.

4. Sir Robert Anderson, *The Silence of God*, 100.

5. Sir Robert Anderson, *Redemption Truths*, 152.

Chapter 4

Justification and Righteousness

On the subjects of "justification" and "righteousness" Sir Robert writes that there are two aspects in regard to "righteousness":

"Righteousness is a complex word. It expresses either a personal moral quality or a judicial state. If any one be personally righteous, he is, of course, and by virtue of it, judicially righteous also. On the other hand, to declare a person to be judicially righteous who personally is 'not' righteous, is, according to human judgment, unrighteous and immoral. But God has done this very thing...the great marvel of the gospel, the great triumph of redemption, is that God can declare those to be righteous who personally are not righteous; that He can justify the sinner, not by deeming him a law-keeper, but even while He judges him as a law-breaker." [1]

The Mystery of the Gospel

According to Sir Robert the great marvel of the gospel is also the "mystery" of the gospel--that God can justify a sinner:

"The mystery of the gospel is that God can justify a sinner, and yet be just. He justifies the ungodly. 'To him that worketh not, but believeth in Him that justifieth the ungodly, his faith is counted for righteousness' (Rom. iv. 5)." [2]

Anderson understands that God can justify the sinner even though He judges him a law-breaker. The Greek word translated "justified" means:

"To declare, pronounce, one to be just, righteous, or such as he ought to be." [3]

God can declare a person to be righteous or just even though that person is not personally righteous. Anderson explains the three basic principles in regard to the justification of the law-breaker:

"GRACE is the characteristic truth of Christianity. According to the great doctrinal treatise of the New Testament, we are 'justified by grace,' 'justified by faith,' 'justified by blood'...Grace is the principle on which God justifies a sinner; faith is the principle on which the benefit is received; and the death of Christ is the ground on which alone all this is possible - we are 'justified freely by His grace through the redemption that is in Christ Jesus.'" [4]

I. Justified by Blood

"For the wages of sin is death..." (Ro.6:23).

In regard to this verse as it applies to "justification by blood" Anderson writes:

"The sentence upon sin is death. Man has fallen beneath that sentence; he is hopelessly, irretrievably doomed. No law-keeping therefore could bring him righteousness: if he is ever to be justified, it must be by the penalty being borne. He must be justified by death, 'justified by blood' (Rom. v. 9)." [5]

Next Sir Robert explains that God imputes the death of Christ to the believer:

"One poem may not constitute a man a poet, but one murder makes a man a murderer, one sin makes a sinner. Nothing but the gallows can expiate a murder; death alone can atone for sin...This is the natural state of the sinner under law. But here God reveals himself a Saviour. He gives up His Only-begotten Son to take the place of the condemned sinner, and die in his

*stead. He now points to that death as satisfying the righteous de-
mand of law against the sinner, and on that ground He justifies
him. Not that by virtue of His sovereignty, or by a legal fiction, as
we say, He reckons the believer to be righteous while leaving his
condition in fact unchanged, but that He 'justifies' him. The believer is 'justified from all things from which he could not be justified by the law of Moses' (Acts xiii. 39). God imputes the death of
Christ to the believer."* [6]

II. Justified by Grace

*"For by grace are ye saved through faith; and that not of
yourselves: it is the gift of God: Not of works, lest any man should
boast"* (Eph.2:8-9).

In his commentary of these verses Anderson writes:

*" 'By grace are ye saved, through faith.' But error is so insidi-
ous and so vital that the Scripture does not stop at a positive
statement of the truth, but adds the words, 'and that (salvation)
not of yourselves, it is the gift of God; not of works, lest any man
should boast.' To speak of 'earning' a gift would be a contradic-
tion in terms; but though a gift can not be earned by works, it
may be 'deserved' on that ground. Men's gifts, indeed, are seldom
bestowed upon the undeserving. Therefore it is that they so often
give ground for boasting. But salvation is not only unearned, but
undeserved; it is not only a gift, but a gift 'by grace.' "* [7]

Indeed, Paul declares in no uncertain terms that "grace" is di-
ametrically opposed to "works":

*"For if Abraham were justified by works, he hath whereof to
glory; but not before God. For what saith the scripture? Abraham
believed God, and it was counted unto him for righteousness.
Now to him that worketh is the reward not reckoned of grace, but
of debt"* (Ro.4:2-4).

If anyone receives a reward based on any "work" then it cannot be said that the reward is according to the principle of

"grace." Next, Anderson explains that no limit can be placed on grace:

"But if grace be on the throne, what limits can be set to it? If that sin committed upon Calvary has not shut the door of mercy, all other sins together shall not avail to close it. If God can bless in spite of the death of Christ, who may not be blest? Innocence lost, conscience disobeyed and stifled, covenants and promises despised and forfeited, law trampled under foot, prophets persecuted, and last and unutterably terrible, the Only-begotten slain. And yet there is mercy still!...As surely as the sin of man brought death, the grace of God shall bring eternal life to every sinner who believes. One sin brought death, but grace masters 'all' sin. If sin abounded, grace abounds far more. Grace is conqueror. GRACE REIGNS." [8]

III. Justified by Faith

In regard to the third and final principle Anderson writes:

"Grace implies that there is no merit in him who is the object of it, no reason whatever in him why he should be blessed. How then, if the blessing be not arbitrarily limited, if it be really unto all, can a difference be made? how can one be justified and another not? It cannot depend on merit; it cannot depend on effecting a change in one's self; it cannot depend on doing. It must be simply that one accepts and another rejects a righteousness which is perfect independently of the sinner. How accepts ? how rejects? accepts by believing, rejects by disbelieving, the testimony of God. 'Unto all and upon all them that believe.' 'It is of faith that it may be by grace' : any other ground would be inconsistent with grace. A sinner must be 'justified by faith' (Rom. v. 1)." [9]

Sir Robert continues on the subject of faith, writing that believing the "good news" of the Lord Jesus brings life:

"In its first and simplest phase in Scripture, faith is the belief of a record or testimony...Faith then in its simplest character is not trust, nor even faith in a person, but belief of a record...The

gospel is not a promise or a covenant, but a message, a procla-
mation. It is the 'good news of God, concerning His Son Jesus
Christ our Lord.' And the belief of that good news is life." [10]

Certainly no one could construe the following words of Sir
Robert as referring to a blind faith:

" 'The rational attitude of a thinking mind towards the super-
natural is that of skepticism'... But if GOD speaks, then skepticism
gives place to faith. Nor is this a mere begging of the question.
The proof that the voice is really Divine must be absolute and
conclusive. In such circumstances, skepticism betokens mental or
moral degradation, and faith is not the abnegation of reason, but
the highest act of reason. To maintain that such proof is impossi-
ble, is equivalent to asserting that the God who made us cannot
so speak to us that the voice shall carry with it the conviction that
it is from Him; and this is not skepticism at all, but disbelief and
atheism." [11]

With that in mind it is not surprising to hear Anderson say that
the Christian is not in doubt concerning the revelation he has received:

"The Christian is not ignorant; neither is he in doubt. We do
not 'think' this or that: we KNOW. 'We know that the Son of God
is come.' 'We know that He was manifested to take away our sins.'
'We know that we have passed from death unto life.' 'We know
that if our earthly house were dissolved, we have a building of
God, eternal in the heavens.' 'We know that when He shall appear
we shall be like Him.'" [12]

Speaking of "faith" Anderson says that faith is *"the conviction*
of things not seen":

"We are saved by faith; and faith is the reception, as true, of
what is beyond the range of proof, either by demonstration or by
evidence. It is the substance (or assurance) of things hoped or
trusted for, the conviction of things not seen (Heb. xi. 9)." [13]

That being true the Christian knows that God has given him an understanding that these things are true:

"And we know that the Son of God is come, and hath given us an understanding, that we may know Him that is true, and we are in Him that is true, even in his Son Jesus Christ. This is the true God, and eternal life" (1Jn.5:20).

Summary

Here we read a summation of Anderson's argument in regard to "justification":

"The sinner, then, is 'justified by grace,' because God can find no reason, no motive, save in His own heart, for blessing him at all. He is 'justified by faith,' because this is the only principle of blessing consistent with grace. And, thirdly, he is 'justified by blood,' because the stern facts of Divine righteousness and human sin make blessing impossible, save on the ground of redemption." [14]

Next we will examine the basic truths that surround the teaching of "redemption."

NOTES

1. Sir Robert Anderson, *The Gospel And Its Ministry*, 109-110.

2. Sir Robert Anderson, *The Silence of God*, 201.

3. Joseph Henry Thayer, *A Greek-English Lexicon of the New Testament*, 150.

4. Sir Robert Anderson, *The Silence of God*, 99.

5. Sir Robert Anderson, *The Gospel And Its Ministry*, 101.

6. *Ibid.,* 164-165.

7. Sir Robert Anderson, *Redemption Truths*, 91-92.

8. Sir Robert Anderson, *The Gospel And Its Ministry*, 17-19.

9. *Ibid.,* 101-102.

10. *Ibid.,* 39, 42-43.

11. Sir Robert Anderson, *The Coming Prince,* 10-11.

12. Sir Robert Anderson, *The Gospel And Its Ministry*, x.

13. *Ibid.,* 52-53.

14. Sir Robert Anderson, *Redemption Truths*, 84-85.

Chapter 5

Redemption

One of the Greek words translated "redemption" in the New Testament is *apolytrōsis* and that word means:

> *"A releasing effected by payment of ransom, deliverance."* [1]

The believer is released or delivered from a spiritual death sentence because the Lord Jesus gave Himself a ransom for all:

> *"For there is one God, and one mediator between God and men, the man Christ Jesus; Who gave himself a ransom for all"* (1 Tim.2:6).

On the subject of the "ransom" Anderson writes that

> *"Most true it is that Christ 'gave Himself a ransom for all'; but redemption includes not merely the payment of the ransom but the deliverance of the ransomed."* [2]

Redemption Includes Both Righteousness and Sanctification

Redemption includes both a righteous standing before God as well as "sanctification":

> *"Of Him are ye in Christ Jesus, who was made unto us wisdom from God, and both righteousness and sanctification, even redemption"* (1 Cor.1:30; R.V. margin).

Anderson writes that a Christian's redemption includes not only relief from wrath but also access to the Lord's presence:

"He is 'made unto us wisdom, and both righteousness and sanctification, even redemption'-- redemption in its fulness as including all we need, not only to secure relief from wrath, but to bring us into covenant relationship with God, and to give us access to His presence." [3]

The ultimate purpose of redemption is to give the believer access into the presence of God. Sir Robert writes:

"If God is the Saviour of His people, He has a purpose toward them in salvation. 'I bare you on eagles' wings and brought you to Myself,' was His word to Israel, and such is the great end and aim of the work of Christ to usward. God would have His people near Him. The death of Christ was 'to bring us unto God.' By that blood we are 'made nigh.' " [4]

We have already shown how the believer is "declared righteous" or "justified" before God. Sir Robert writes that justification itself can give no one fitness to approach a holy God:

"The release of a person who stands charged with an offence, gives him neither right nor fitness to approach his Sovereign, much less to live in the palace; and no such gulf separates a king from his meanest subject as that which yawns between a sinner and a thrice-holy God. Forgiveness of sins could give neither title nor fitness to draw near to the Divine Majesty. It might ensure exemption from hell, but it certainly could give no right to heaven. But redemption is more than mere forgiveness. Christ satisfies the sinner's need in all its variety and depth." [5]

Sanctification

Anderson explains the relationship of "sin" in regard to both "justification" and "sanctification" in the following way:

"Sin...has a relation both to righteousness and to holiness, but, essentially, it is 'lawlessness' : lawlessness and sin are synonymous terms. The answer to the guilt of sin is justification, and

to its defilement, sanctification. In virtue of the blood we are both justified and sanctified." [6]

He then explains that the sinner is sanctified in the same way that he is justified:

"By nature not righteous but guilty, we have seen how the sinner is justified. By nature not holy but defiled, he is likewise sanctified. And both depend alike, and only, upon blood. He is righteous, moreover, because God has declared him righteous; and it is by the call of God that he is holy. 'And such were some of you,' the apostle reminds the Corinthian Christians, after naming transgressors of the grossest kind, 'but ye are washed, but ye are sanctified, but ye are justified' (1 Cor. vi. 11) : 'Sanctified in Christ Jesus, called saints,' (1 Cor. i. 2) as he had described them in the salutation of the epistle." [7]

Here is the verse to which Anderson makes reference:

"To the assembly of God which is in Corinth, to those sanctified in Christ Jesus, called saints, with all that in every place call on the name of our Lord Jesus Christ, both theirs and ours" (1 Cor.1:2; DBY).

The believer is a saint "in virtue of his redemption," as Anderson explains:

"The Corinthians, to whom these words are written, are addressed by the Apostle as 'them that are sanctified in Christ Jesus, called saints.' Not 'called to be saints,' but saints by their calling. To become a saint is the effort of the religionist; but the redeemed sinner is a saint in virtue of his redemption. The struggle of the religionist is to 'become what he is not'; the aim of the Christian is to realize 'what he is' - to 'walk worthy of the calling wherewith he is called.' 'Saints and sinners' is an ignorant and false antithesis; for every saint is a sinner, though every sinner is not a saint." [8]

According to Sir Robert *"sanctification in this sense, therefore, is not a gradual change"*:

"Sanctification in this sense, therefore, is not a gradual change or a progressive work, nor yet a moral attribute ; it is an act, like justification, accomplished once for all. Just as the guilty sinner passes, immediately when he believes, into a new condition relatively to sin and a righteous God, and becomes thereby and thenceforth righteous; so the defiled sinner gains, as immediately and in the same way, a new standing relatively to sin and a holy God, and becomes thereby and thenceforth holy.

'Whatsoever God doeth, it shall be for ever: nothing can be put to it, nor anything taken from it'
(Eccles. iii. 14)." [9]

Here are the verses which demonstrates that sanctification in regard to a believer's standing in Christ is accomplished once for all:

"By the which will we are sanctified through the offering of the body of Jesus Christ once for all...For by one offering he hath perfected for ever them that are sanctified" (Heb.10:10,14).

Anderson then states the practical principles in regard to sanctification:

"The Divine grace which freely justifies a sinner, and then teaches him to live righteously, also sanctifies and teaches him to live holily. He does not live righteously in order to become justified, but because he has been justified; neither does he live holily in order to become sanctified, but because he has been sanctified. And as he is justified, so also is he sanctified, by the blood of Christ (Heb. x. 29)." [10]

Anderson concludes his remarks on redemption by writing the following:

" 'He' is our sanctification. The words are plain and simple: 'But of Him are ye in Christ Jesus who was made unto us wisdom

from God, and both righteousness and sanctification, even re-
demption.' It is only in virtue of what Christ has done for us that
we can gain the place we hold in redemption.” [11]

NOTES

1. Joseph Henry Thayer, *A Greek-English Lexicon of the New Testament*, 65.

2. Sir Robert Anderson, *Redemption Truths*, 88.

3. Sir Robert Anderson, *Misunderstood Texts of the New Testament*, 84.

4. Sir Robert Anderson, *The Gospel And Its Ministry*, 136.

5. Sir Robert Anderson, *Redemption Truths*, 37.

6. Sir Robert Anderson, *The Gospel And Its Ministry*, 180.

7. *Ibid.,* 121.

8. Sir Robert Anderson, *Redemption Truths*, 86-87.

9. Sir Robert Anderson, *The Gospel And Its Ministry*, 121-122.

10. Sir Robert Anderson, *Redemption Truths*, 87.

11. Sir Robert Anderson, *The Gospel And Its Ministry*, 172.

Chapter 6

Redemption in "Type"

Introduction to "Types"

God has given us a series of pictures or illustrations from the Old Testament and a close examination of these "types" can give us a clear understanding of certain spiritual truths which apply to us.

In one of her many books examining the Old Testament "types" Ada R. Habershon quotes Robert Anderson saying that *"the typology of the old Testament is the very alphabet of the language in which the doctrine of the New Testament is written; and as many of our great theologians are admittedly ignorant of the typology, we need not feel surprised if they are not always the safest exponents of the doctrines." [1]*

Habershon stresses the importance of the study of "types" by saying that *"the Inspiration of the Scriptures is attacked on all sides; the doctrine of Atonement by substitution is denied, or thought little of; whilst other things are preached which are contrary to the Word. This could not be so frequenty the case if the Old Testament types were more carefully studied and more widely taught." [2]*

Now let us look at an OT passage which speaks of "types":

"For I would not have you ignorant, brethren, that all our fathers were under the cloud, and all passed through the sea...But these things happened as types of us" (1 Cor.10:1:6; DBY).

Miss Habershon explains that these types were given to us to teach us certain lessons:

"It is very important to understand what is meant by a type. In I Cor. x. we are told concerning the various wilderness experiences of the children of Israel, that 'all these things happened unto them for types'; and Paul explains that the record of these events is given to us in the Bible for a special purpose, viz., to teach us certain lessons. This passage seems to cover all that befell God's redeemed people in their journey from the place of bondage to the land of promise; and we may also conclude from it that other portions of their history are given to us for a similar purpose." [3]

Sir Robert refers to the same passage and says that the story of Israel's history is rich in typical teaching:

"Now, these things, we are expressly told, were 'types'...Every part of the wonderful story, indeed, is rich in typical teaching. The manna from heaven for their food was a type of Christ. The rock that gave out water for their thirst was a type of Christ." [4]

The Greek word *typos* is translated "type" and in a doctrinal sense a "type" is defined the following way:

"A person or thing prefiguring a future (Messianic) person or thing." [5]

An example of one of the "types" mentioned at 1 Corinthians 10 is in regard to the "spiritual food":

"They were all baptized into Moses in the cloud and in the sea. They all ate the same spiritual food and drank the same spiritual drink..." (1 Cor.10:2-3; NIV).

The "spiritual food" refers to the supernatural manna that rained down from heaven after the children of Israel crossed the Red Sea and were in the wilderness of Shur:

"And when the children of Israel saw it, they said one to another, It is manna: for they wist not what it was. And Moses said unto them, This is the bread which the LORD hath given you to eat" (Ex.16:15).

This "manna" which fell around the camp of Israel is a "type" and the "anti-type" (that which fulfills or is illustrated by the type) is the Lord Jesus, as witnessed by His words here:

"My Father giveth you the true bread from heaven; for the bread of God is he which cometh down from heaven, and giveth life unto the world" (Jn.6:33-34).

The manna from heaven provides an illustration from the physical sphere that pictures certain truths in the spiritual sphere. Just as the manna from heaven gave physical life to the children of Israel the Lord Jesus gives spiritual life to all who believe.

"Types" in Regard to a Believer's Redemption

The record of the many events which the "nation" of Israel experienced in regard to her "redemption" prefigured and illustrates the "individual" Christian's "redemption":

"And what one nation in the earth is like thy people, even like Israel, whom God went to redeem for a people to himself, and to make him a name, and to do for you great things and terrible, for thy land, before thy people, which thou redeemedst to thee from Egypt, from the nations and their gods?" (2 Sam.7:23).

In a lecture given at Dallas Theological Seminary on the subject of "typology" Charles T. Fritsch stated that *"the exodus, the deliverance of a nation, becomes a type of the redemptive work of Christ--also clearly adumbrated in the exile--where the individual is brought to realize his own tremendous guilt and need of redemption."* [6]

From this we can understand that the redemption of the "nation" of Israel serves as a "type" which illustrates the redemptive work of Christ in regard to "individuals." Sir Robert says that by studying the "types" we may learn in its fullness what the redemption of Christ has won for us:

"No one must suppose, of course, that the blessings prefigured by the types come to the believer in a chronological sequence, or that they are separated by intervals of time. But in the key-pictures these stages are clearly distinguished, in order that our minds may dwell upon them, and that thus we may learn in all its fullness what the redemption of Christ has won for us." [7]

I. Justification in "Type"

Here Anderson states that the history of Israel in its typical character began when they were in bondage in Egypt:

"The narrative of Genesis closes by recording how the descendants of Abraham came to be sojourners in the land of Egypt. As we turn the page, the opening chapter of Exodus tells how they had lapsed into a condition of hard and degrading servitude. This is the point at which the history of Israel in its 'typical' character begins. Man's condition by nature is that of slavery in the house of bondage. He is absolutely dependent on a Divine deliverer." [8]

In "type" the Israelites were slaves to the Egyptians and this state of slavery illustrates a man's condition as being a slave to sin:

"When you were slaves to sin, you were free from the control of righteousness" (Ro.6:20; NIV).

Next we see in type that a "death sentence" from God was issued against all the first born living in Egypt:

"And all the firstborn in the land of Egypt shall die, from the first born of Pharaoh that sitteth upon his throne, even unto the firstborn of the maidservant that is behind the mill; and all the firstborn of beasts" (Ex.11:5).

According to Anderson this death sentence is a "key-picture" of the Christian's redemption story:

"The key-picture of our redemption story is perfect even in details. Being in Egypt, they came under Egypt's doom; for in the types the first-born represented the family, and the Divine decree was that 'all the first-born in the land of Egypt shall die.' There was no exemption for Israel." [9]

The death sentence that is illustrated by the "type" is seen as being as a result of sin:

"Don't you know that when you offer yourselves to someone to obey him as slaves, you are slaves to the one whom you obey— whether you are slaves to sin, which leads to death, or to obedience, which leads to righteousness?" (Ro.6:16; NIV).

This death is a "spiritual" death and not a "physical" one, as witnessed by the Lord's words to Adam and Eve:

"And the LORD God commanded the man, saying, Of every tree of the garden thou mayest freely eat: But of the tree of the knowledge of good and evil, thou shalt not eat of it: for in the day that thou eatest thereof thou shalt surely die" (Gen.2:16-17).

Both Adam and Eve died spiritually on the day that they ate of the forbidden fruit. A "death" is properly defined as a "separation." A "physical" death is a separation between the physical body and the soul. A "spiritual" death is the separation between the soul and the Spirit of God. Anderson describes the primary death which the Lord Jesus experienced on the Cross as being a separation from God:

"The cup which the Father had given Him to drink was death in its primary and deepest sense, as separation from God. Scripture speaks of it as His 'being made a curse for us.'" [10]

Here we see the Lord Jesus being "forsaken" by the Father at the Cross and therefore at that moment a separation between the Two took place:

"And at the ninth hour Jesus cried with a loud voice, saying, Eloi, Eloi, lama sabachthani? which is, being interpreted, My God, my God, why hast thou forsaken me?" (Mk.15:34).

Returning to the "types," Anderson says that a death sentence went out upon all of the inhabitants in Egypt and this death sentence can only be satisfied by death:

"This was not a sentence upon the 'Egyptians,' but upon the inhabitants of the land. The doom fell upon Egypt and upon all who dwelt in Egypt. There was no difference here between the Israelite and the Egyptian. And a death sentence can be satisfied only by death. But God provided a redemption." [11]

Next Sir Robert explains how God provided a redemption:

"The story of the Passover is known to all. Every Hebrew family was to sacrifice a lamb, and the blood of that sacrifice was to be sprinkled upon the lintel and the door-posts of every Hebrew hut. For the Divine word declared, 'I will pass through the land of Egypt this night, and will smite all the firstborn in the land if Egypt. . . . And when I see the blood I will pass over you.' Or, as Moses explained it to the people, 'The Lord will pass over the door, and will not suffer the destroyer to come into your houses to smite you.' Death was the appointed judgment upon Egypt; but upon the blood-stained house death had already passed." [12]

Anderson explains that the blood which was sprinkled upon the dwellings brought the Israelites deliverance from the death sentence:

"The blood of the Passover, sprinkled upon the dwellings of the Israelites, brought them deliverance from the death judgment passed upon Egypt...The demands of Divine righteousness had been satisfied before their deliverance from Egypt...they had...been justified by the blood of the Passover." [13]

The children of Israel had been justified or made right with God by the blood of the passover lambs in Israel. The Passover lambs are a "type" which illustrate the principles in regard to the believer's justification by the blood of the "antitype," the Lord Jesus Christ:

"Purge out therefore the old leaven, that ye may be a new lump, as ye are unleavened. For even Christ our passover is sacrificed for us" (1 Cor.5:7).

The Israelites escaped the death sentence when they were justified by blood. Anderson observes that this teaches the truth that the sinner must be saved as he is and where he is:

"THE story of the Passover teaches the great truth that salvation is God's work altogether, and that a sinner can be saved only through redemption. And it teaches the further truth that he must be saved as he is and where he is, in his ruin and helplessness and guilt. If a sinner could not be saved 'in his sins,' salvation would be impossible, for there is no power of recovery in him. But this is only the beginning. God alone can take him out of the horrible pit and out of the miry clay. But God does do this, and He sets his feet upon a rock, and establishes his goings, and puts a new song in his mouth." [14]

Next we will look at the "types" in regard to the nation's exit out of Egypt. Anderson says:

"The redemption 'in' Egypt was followed by redemption 'from' Egypt. The sinner is 'saved in his sins,' but that is not all: he is saved 'from his sins.' Israel's redemption in Egypt was only and altogether by the blood of the lamb: redemption from Egypt was by 'the strong hand and the outstretched arm' of Israel's God. The passage of the sea was the first in that wonderful journey. 'The waters divided,' and the redeemed people passed through as on dry land. But when the Egyptians press after them, the waters returned and overwhelmed them." [15]

The "type" of Israel's exit out of Egypt illustrates the truth that the power of sin has been broken in regard to believers. Anderson writes:

"Redemption by blood, was followed by redemption by power. With a strong hand were they brought out, and their deliverance was not complete until they stood upon the wilderness-side of the sea, and saw their enemies dead upon the shore - saw the power that had enslaved them broken." [16]

The Apostle Paul speaks of this enslaving power of sin being broken:

"For sin shall not have dominion over you: for ye are not under the law, but under grace" (Ro.6:14).

The Greek word *kyrieuō* is translated "dominion" and that word means *"to have power over...Ro. vi. 14."* [17]

The Apostle Paul says that the Christian has been "set free from sin":

"But thanks be to God that, though you used to be slaves to sin, you wholeheartedly obeyed the form of teaching to which you were entrusted. You have been set free from sin and have become slaves to righteousness" (Ro.6:17-18; NIV).

II. Sanctification in "Type"

Anderson next explains the situation of the Israelites after they were redeemed out of Egypt:

"A few weeks only had passed since the Israelites had groaned in Egyptian bondage: now they stood a redeemed people around Mount Sinai, and God had given them a law, and prescribed for them a religion. But while His purpose was to have His people near Him, the scene only emphasised the distance which separated them from Him. Great and wonderful though the blessings were which they had already proved, their redemption was wholly incomplete." [18]

Sir Robert next speaks of the distance that separated God from His people even after they had been redeemed out of Egypt:

"Warning after warning was given them not to come near to Him. They must not touch even the base of the mountain on which He was about to manifest His presence. His command to Moses was, 'Go down, charge the people, lest they break through unto the Lord to gaze, and many of them perish' (Exodus xix.12,13,21,24). Moses, who typified 'the Mediator of the New Covenant,' might approach; but as for the people, they were warned off at the peril of their lives." [19]

Next Moses set up an altar and the sacrifice of the covenant was offered. Anderson writes,

"When Moses had thus received 'all the words of the Lord and all the judgments,' he came and told them to the people, and then recorded them in writing. This accomplished, he set up an altar, and the great sacrifice of the covenant was offered; and by the blood of that sacrifice, sprinkled both upon the book and upon the people, the covenant was dedicated. in other words, Israel was thus brought into covenant with God, and became a holy people, as befitted the relationship." [20]

Sir Robert then explains the amazing change that took place after the nation of Israel was sanctified by the blood of the covenant:

"The blood of the covenant sacrifices was sprinkled, on the people - the elders presumably representing the whole congregation of Israel - and then we read, Aaron and the elders ascended the mountain along with Moses. But yesterday it would have been death to them to 'break through to gaze.' But now 'they saw God.' And such was their 'boldness,' due to the blood of the covenant, that 'they did eat and drink' in the divine presence." [21]

Anderson continues, pointing out the "typical" relationship between Moses as mediator and the Lord Jesus as our heavenly Mediator:

"What was the next step in the typical story of redemption? By the sprinkling of the blood of the covenant Israel was sanctified;

and then, to the very people who were warned against daring to draw near to God, the command was given, 'Let them make Me a sanctuary that I may dwell among them' (Exodus xxv. 8). Moses, the mediator of the covenant, having thus made purification of the sins of the people, went up to God. This was the type, the shadow, of which we have in Hebrews the fulfillment, the reality; for when the Son of God 'had made purification of sins' 'by the blood of the everlasting covenant,' he went up to God, and 'sat down on the right hand of the Majesty on high' (Hebrews i. 3; cf. xiii. 20)." [22]

As a result of being sanctified by the blood the Christian now has an High Priest in heaven so therefore he is urged to come boldly to the throne of grace:

"For we have not an high priest which cannot be touched with the feeling of our infirmities; but was in all points tempted like as we are, yet without sin. Let us therefore come boldly unto the throne of grace, that we may obtain mercy, and find grace to help in time of need" (Heb.4:15-16).

NOTES

1. Ada R. Habershon, *Study of the Types* (Grand Rapids: Kregel Publications, 1993), 10-11.

2. *Ibid.,* 10.

3. *Ibid.,* 11.

4. Sir Robert Anderson, *The Bible or the Church?* 183.

5. Joseph Henry Thayer, *A Greek-English Lexicon of the New Testament*, 632.

6. Charles T. Fritsch, "Principles of Biblical Typology," *Bibliotheca Sacra*, 104 (April-June, 1947), 220.

7. Sir Robert Anderson, *Redemption Truths*, 28.

8. Sir Robert Anderson, *The Bible or the Church?* 179.

9. Sir Robert Anderson, *Redemption Truths*, 24.

10. *Ibid.,* 116.

11. Sir Robert Anderson, *The Bible or the Church?* 180.

12. *Ibid.,* 180-181.

13. Sir Robert Anderson, *Misunderstood Texts of the New Testament*, 83-84.

14. Sir Robert Anderson, *Redemption Truths*, 35.

15. Sir Robert Anderson, *The Bible or the Church?* 182.

16. Sir Robert Anderson, *Redemption Truths*, 35-36.

17. Joseph Henry Thayer, *A Greek-English Lexicon of the New Testament*, 365.

18. Sir Robert Anderson, *The Bible or the Church?* 184.

19. Sir Robert Anderson, *Redemption Truths*, 38.

20. Sir Robert Anderson, *The Bible or the Church?* 185.

21. Sir Robert Anderson, *Types in Hebrews,* 19.

22. *Ibid.,* 20.

Chapter 7

Christic as High Priest

Anderson speaks of two different priesthoods, one being earthly and the other being heavenly:

"While the old covenant had an earthly sanctuary and a human priesthood, the sanctuary of the new covenant is heaven itself, and the Great Priest who ministers there is no other than the Son of God." [1]

The following verses describe the duties of the earthly priests on the "Day of Atonement":

"For on that day shall the priest make an atonement for you, to cleanse you, that ye may be clean from all your sins before the LORD...And this shall be an everlasting statute unto you, to make an atonement for the children of Israel for all their sins once a year" (Lev.16:30,34).

Commenting on these duties Sir Robert says:

The priest was 'appointed for men in things pertaining to God,' and one of his chief functions was 'to make an atonement for the children of Israel, for all their sins.'" [2]

It is also important to understand that these services were for a people already redeemed by blood. Anderson says:

"The book of Leviticus is based upon the book of Exodus. The offerings it prescribes are for a people who stand in the liberty and joy of redemption." [3]

The Scriptures also reveal that the Lord Jesus is now our High Priest and in that role He is also making atonement for sins:

"For this reason he had to be made like his brothers in every way, in order that he might become a merciful and faithful high priest in service to God, and that he might make atonement for the sins of the people" (Heb.2:17; NIV).

Anderson quotes this verse and then remarks:

"This is not redemption for a lost world, but atonement for the sins of a redeemed people." [4]

Although the earthly priesthood was similar to the one of the Lord Jesus in certain respects it is also different in other important ways. Anderson writes:

"That the priesthood of Christ could not be Aaronic, the Apostle impresses on the Jewish mind by pointing to the fact that 'our Lord sprang out of Judah, of which tribe Moses spake nothing concerning priesthood.' And the truth in question is made 'still more evident,' he adds, by the fact that the Lord's priesthood was divinely declared to be of the order of Melchisedek. That Melchisedek was type of the Messiah the Jews themselves admitted; and his priesthood had to do, not with offering sacrifices for sins, but with ministering blessing and succour and sustenance." [5]

Expanding on the Lord's duties as High Priest Sir Robert says:

"He is at the right hand of God, to make atonement and intercession for us, and to sympathize and succour in all the needs and trials of our chequered life...His present work of atonement and intercession are not needed to appease an alienated Diety, nor to overcome divine unwillingness to bless a sinner. But He thus makes it possible for God to bless us consistently with all that He is, and all that He has declared Himself to be." [6]

The result of the atonement of our High Priest is the same as that of the earthly priesthood on the day of atonement--to cleanse those who are already redeemed from the defilement caused by sin:

"For on that day shall the priest make an atonement for you, to cleanse you, that ye may be clean from all your sins before the LORD" (Lev.16:30).

The result is to cleanse those already redeemed from sins, the same thing spoken of here:

"If we say that we have fellowship with him, and walk in darkness, we lie, and do not the truth: But if we walk in the light, as he is in the light, we have fellowship one with another, and the blood of Jesus Christ his Son cleanseth us from all sin. If we say that we have no sin, we deceive ourselves, and the truth is not in us. If we confess our sins, he is faithful and just to forgive us our sins, and to cleanse us from all unrighteousness" (1 Jn.1:6-9).

According to the Apostle John it is "confession" that results in cleansing:

"The blood of Jesus Christ his Son cleanseth us from all sin...If we confess our sins, he is faithful and just to forgive us our sins, and to cleanse us from all unrighteousness."

Commenting on these words Sir Robert says:

"For the believer who sins against God to dismiss the matter by 'the blood cleanseth,' is the levity and daring of antinomianism. For such the word is, 'If we confess our sins': no flippant acknowledgment with the lip, but a solemn and real dealing with God; and thus he obtains again and again a renewal of the benefits of the death of Christ. 'He is faithful and just to forgive us our sins and to cleanse us from all unrighteousness.' " [7]

Anderson also says the following about confession:

"If we yield to sin and have recourse to evil practices, we need not look to Him for 'sympathy,' though a penitent confession will bring pardon full and free through His atoning work. But an in-

citement or tendency to evil if resisted and kept down is reckoned an 'infirmity,' and we can look with confidence to One who can be 'touched with the feeling of our infirmities' - to One who in doing the will of God has suffered as we have never suffered, as we, with our fallen nature, are incapable of suffering." [8]

Next, Anderson sums up the amazing facts concerning our High Priest:

"That the Son of God - He who was with God, and was God, the brightness of His glory and the express image of His person, He who upholds all things by the word of His power - came down to earth to take part of flesh and blood, and here to live a life of poverty and suffering and reproach, 'despised and rejected of men,' and to die a death of infamy as a common malefactor; and that now, with 'all power in heaven and on earth,' He is at the right hand of God, to make atonement and intercession for us, and to sympathize and succour in all the needs and trials of our chequered life - if men were not so superstitious and stupid in the religious sphere, this would divide the world into two hostile camps, and every one would become either a devout worshipper or an open infidel. For in all the fables of the false religions of the world there is nothing so utterly incredible as this." [9]

NOTES

1. Sir Robert Anderson, *Types in Hebrews,* 57.

2. Sir Robert Anderson, *The Gospel And Its Ministry*, 188.

3. *Ibid.,* 189.

4. *Ibid.,* 188.

5. Sir Robert Anderson, *Types in Hebrews,* 29.

6. *Ibid.,* 61-62.

7. Sir Robert Anderson, *The Gospel And Its Ministry*, 177.

8. Sir Robert Anderson, *Types in Hebrews,* 67-68.

9. *Ibid.,* 60-61.

Chapter 8

Regeneration – Being Born Again

Here the Apostle Paul speaks of those being "dead" having been made "alive":

"And you hath he made alive, who were dead in trespasses and sins" (Eph.2:1).

A sinner's "regeneration" or being "born again" is accomplished by the word of God and the Spirit, as witnessed by what the Lord Jesus says here:

"The Spirit gives life; the flesh counts for nothing. The words I have spoken to you are spirit and they are life" (Jn.6:63; NIV).

Anderson says that Peter's faith was not based on the miracles which He saw the Lord Jesus perform but instead was based on a revelation which he received from the heavenly Father:

"St. Peter was one of the favored three who witnessed every miracle, including the transfiguration, and yet his faith was not the result of these, but sprang from a revelation to himself. In response to his confession, 'Thou art the Christ, the Son of the living God,' the Lord declared, 'Flesh and blood hath not revealed it unto thee, but my Father who is in heaven' (Matt. xvi. 16,17). Nor, again, was this a special grace accorded only to apostles. 'To them that have obtained like precious faith with us' (2 Peter i. 1), was St. Peter's address to the faithful generally. He describes them as 'born again by the Word of God' (1 Peter i. 23). So also St. John speaks of such as 'born, not of blood, nor of the will of the flesh, nor of the will of man, but of God' (John i. 13). 'Of His

own will begat He us with the word of truth' is the kindred state-ment of St. James (James i. 18). Whatever be the meaning of such words, they must mean something more than arriving at a sound conclusion from sufficient premises, or accepting facts upon suf-ficient evidence. Nor will it avail to urge that this birth was mere-ly the mental or moral change naturally caused by the truth thus attained by natural means. The language of the Scripture is une-quivocal that the power of the testimony to produce this change depended on the presence and operation of God." [1]

We can see that the testimony depends on the operation of God, specifically the power of the Holy Spirit:

"...they spoke of the things that have now been told you by those who have preached the gospel to you by the Holy Spirit sent from heaven" (1 Pet.1:12; NIV).

"...our gospel came to you not simply with words, but also with power, with the Holy Spirit and with deep conviction" (1 Thess.1:5; NIV).

The Apostle Paul described his preaching as being *"with a demonstration of the Spirit's power"*:

"My message and my preaching were not with wise and per-suasive words, but with a demonstration of the Spirit's power" (1 Cor.2:4; NIV).

Anderson says that apart from the work of the Spirit a sinner's salvation is impossible:

"His word is itself the power by which dead souls are born again to God. The love of God to man, and the cross of Christ which manifests that love, and the inspired page which contains the record of it, would all be of no avail to save a single sinner, were it not for the Spirit's work." [2]

Sir Robert says that it is by faith that the Spirit is received:

"The Word of God is itself the seed by which we are begotten (1 Pet.i. 23). Faith comes - not by prayer, for there can be no true prayer without it; nor yet by any work of the Spirit in the soul, apart from the message which He brings - faith comes by hearing, and it is by the hearing of faith that the Spirit is received (Gal. iii. 2)." [3]

Anderson again points out that salvation is impossible apart from the work of the Holy Spirit in the soul:

"Faith is impossible apart from the work of the Holy Spirit in the soul...faith in Christ is a metaphysical achievement so difficult that man is insufficient to accomplish it; but that the heart is utterly apostate, and man's natural condition is that of pure distrust of God. More than this, 'the carnal mind is enmity against God.' Man is capable of the firmest and most implicit faith in himself and in the world - aye, and in the devil too, as will be proved one day; but his whole spiritual being is so utterly estranged from God that not only does he not know Him, but, if left to himself, he is incapable of knowing Him." [4]

Sir Robert says that God works today in the same way that He did centuries ago, speaking to men's hearts by the Holy Spirit:

"And if the new birth and the faith of Christianity were thus produced in the case of persons who received the Gospel immediately from the Apostles, nothing less will avail with us who are separated by eighteen centuries from the witnesses and their testimony. God is with His people still. And He speaks to men's hearts, now, as really as He did in early times; not indeed through inspired Apostles, and still less by dreams or visions, but through the Holy Writings which He Himself inspired; and as the result believers are 'born of God,' and obtain the knowledge of forgiveness of sins and of eternal life. The phenomenon is not a natural one, resulting from the study of the evidences; it is 'supernatural' altogether. 'Thinking minds,' regarding it objectively, may, if they please, maintain towards it what they deem 'a rational attitude;' but at least let them own the fact that there are thousands of credible people who can testify to the reality of the expe-

*rience here spoken of, and further let them recognize that it is en-
tirely in accordance with the teaching of the New Testament."* [5]

Anderson uses the following example of God's revelation to
man to illustrate the source of the Christian's born again experience:

*"In the wildest fables of false religions, there is nothing more
utterly incredible than the story of the life and death of the Son of
God. For one who knows who Jesus was, and what 'the Christ'
means, to believe that Jesus is the Christ is so entirely beyond the
possibilities of human reason that it is proof of a birth from God.
He who believes that Jesus is the Son of God is a man with a supernatural faith, a faith that overcomes the world."* [6]

Here are the verses Anderson uses to support his conclusions:

*"Whosoever believeth that Jesus is the Christ is born of
God...For whatsoever is born of God overcometh the world: and
this is the victory that overcometh the world, even our faith. Who
is he that overcometh the world, but he that believeth that Jesus is
the Son of God?"* (1 Jn.5:1-5).

Anderson's argument in regard to the regeneration of the sinner can be summed up with his words here:

*"Distrust of God was the cause of the creature's fall; how fit-
ting it is, then, that faith in God should be the turning point of his
repentance! It is this very element indeed that makes the Gospel
'the power of God unto salvation to everyone that believeth.' With
nothing to look back to but sin, and nothing to look forward to but
wrath, the sinner, with facts and feelings and experience and log-
ic all against him, accepts God's Word of pardon and peace. And
he receives the blessing, not because he has mastered a syllogism,
but because, like Abraham, he believes God. And he becomes a
changed man, not because he has learned the shibboleths of a
right creed, but because, by the truth of God, received in the
power of the Spirit of God, he has been made 'partaker of the Di-*

vine nature.' He has been 'born again, by the Word of God which liveth and abideth for ever.' " [7]

NOTES

1. Sir Robert Anderson, *The Coming Prince,* 11-12.

2. Sir Robert Anderson, *The Gospel And Its Ministry*, 69.

3. *Ibid.,* 69-70.

4. *Ibid.,* 48-49.

5. Sir Robert Anderson, *The Coming Prince,* 13-14.

6. Sir Robert Anderson, *The Gospel And Its Ministry*, 33.

7. Sir Robert Anderson, *Redemption Truths*, 110-111.

Chapter 9

Regeneration in "Type"

In His sermon to Nicodemus the Lord Jesus spoke of regeneration in connection with the "individual" sinner as well as with the "nation" of Israel. He told Nicodemus:

"I tell you the truth, no one can see the kingdom of God unless he is born again" (Jn.3:3; NIV).

To this Nicodemus asked how he could be born again when he is old, and the Lord Jesus said:

"I tell you the truth, no one can enter the kingdom of God unless he is born of water and the Spirit. Flesh gives birth to flesh, but the Spirit gives birth to spirit" (Jn.3:5-6; NIV).

In these verses the Lord Jesus was speaking of an individual's regeneration but He now begins to speak of the nation of Israel's regeneration. The Lord shifts from using the second person "singular" pronoun "you" to the second person "plural":

"You should not be surprised at my saying, 'You must be born again. The wind blows wherever it pleases. You hear its sound, but you cannot tell where it comes from or where it is going. So it is with everyone born of the Spirit" (Jn.3:7-8; NIV). [1]

Nicodemus still not understand, asking, *"How can these things be?"*

By the Lord's reply we can understand that Nicodemus should have been aware of some truth which spoke of a regeneration by the Spirit:

"Art thou a teacher of Israel, and knoweth not these things?" (v.10).

Nicodemus was reprimanded for his ignorance about the doctrine of which the Lord Jesus was speaking. Anderson writes:

"It is certain that the doctrine here implied ought to have been known to Nicodemus; for the Lord rebuked his ignorance of it. But what is called 'Christian baptism' had not yet been instituted. Even 'the Twelve' knew nothing of it: how then could Nicodemus have known of it? The only baptism then known was that of the Baptist, and that baptism was expressly contrasted with the Spirit's work (Matt. iii. 11). It was a public confession of failure and sin, preparatory to receiving a coming Messiah. But 'Christian baptism' was a public confession of faith in Christ already come and gone back to heaven, and a public submission to the Lordship of Christ on the part of those who professed to have been already 'born of the Spirit.' That is to say, baptism followed the new birth. When Cornelius and his household were brought in, the question was not 'Why should not baptized persons receive the Spirit?' but 'Can any man forbid water that these should not be baptized, who have received the Holy Ghost as well as we?' Their baptism was not the completion of the new birth, but the recognition that they were already born of water and the Spirit." [2]

Anderson continues on this subject by saying that the Lord Jesus was referring to a distinctive truth of the Old Testament:

"Here we must keep prominently in view that the truth involved ought to have been known to Nicodemus. 'Art thou the teacher of Israel, and knowest not these things?' the Lord exclaimed in indignant wonder at his ignorance. Therefore in speaking of the new birth by water and the Spirit the Lord referred to some distinctive truth of the Old Testament Scriptures, which ought to have been familiar to a Rabbi of the Sanhedrin." [3]

Next Anderson says that Nicodemus should have been aware of the prophecy concerning Israel in the book of Ezekiel:

"As already noticed, the Lord's words to Nicodemus referred to some Old Testament Scripture with which he ought to have been familiar. Nor is there any doubt what that Scripture was, namely, Ezekiel xxxvi.- xxxvii., a prophecy that was greatly cherished by the Jew; and ignorance of it would have been as discreditable to a Rabbi as ignorance of the Nicodemus sermon would be to a Christian theologian." 4

In the thirty-seventh chapter of Ezekiel we see the prophet recount that he was taken to a valley which was full of bones:

"The hand of the LORD was upon me, and carried me out in the spirit of the LORD, and set me down in the midst of the valley which was full of bones, And caused me to pass by them round about: and, behold, there were very many in the open valley; and, lo, they were very dry" (Ez.37:1-2).

Later in the prophecy the prophet identifies the "dry bones" as the whole house of Israel:

"Then he said unto me, Son of man, these bones are the whole house of Israel: behold, they say, Our bones are dried, and our hope is lost: we are cut off for our parts" (Ez.37:11).

The following verses from the same prophecy describe how the nation of Israel will be regenerated:

"And he said to me, 'Son of man, can these bones live?' And I answered, 'O Lord God, you know.' Then he said to me, 'Prophesy over these bones, and say to them, O dry bones, hear the word of the Lord. Thus says the Lord God to these bones: Behold, I will cause spirit to enter you, and you shall live. And I will lay sinews upon you, and will cause flesh to come upon you, and cover you with skin, and put spirit in you, and you shall live, and you shall know that I am the Lord' " (Ez.37:3-6; ESV).

Anderson uses these verses to illustrate the Christian's born-again experience:

"You ask, how can sinners, helpless, hopeless, dead - as dead as dry bones scattered upon the earth - be born again to God. 'Can these bones live?' is the question of Ezekiel xxxvii. And the answer comes 'Prophesy unto these bones, and say unto them, O ye dry bones, hear the word of the Lord.' Preach to dead, lost sinners call upon them to hear the word of the Lord. This is man's part. Or if there be anything more, it is, 'Prophesy unto the Breath. Pray that the Spirit may breathe upon these slain that they may live.' The rest is God's work altogether, for 'the Spirit breathes where He wills.' Not that there is anything arbitrary in His working. God is never arbitrary; but He is always Sovereign. Men preach; the Spirit breathes; and the dry bones live. Thus it is that sinners are born again to God." [5]

Sir Robert's following words serve to sum up his remarks about the Christian's regeneration:

"As Scripture declares, 'we are born again by the word of God' - 'the living and eternally abiding word of God.' And to bar all error or mistake, it is added 'And this is the word which by the Gospel is preached unto you' - preached, as the Apostle has already said, 'with the Holy Ghost sent down from heaven.' (1 Peter i. 12, 23, 25). Not the Spirit without the word, nor the word without the Spirit, but the word preached in the power of the Spirit." [6]

NOTES

1. In verse seven the word "you" has a footnote which reads: *"The Greek is plural."*

2. Sir Robert Anderson, *The Bible or the Church?* 223.

3. *Ibid.,* 224.

4. Sir Robert Anderson, *Misunderstood Texts of the New Testament,* 62.

5. Sir Robert Anderson, *Redemption Truths,* 137-138.

6. *Ibid.,* 136-137.

Chapter 10

Self-Judged and Guilty

In this chapter Anderson cites the "types" in regard to "leprosy" to teach the truths about the sinner's self-judgment.

He writes:

"As with the parables, so also with the types; intelligence is needed in deducing the spiritual lessons they are meant to teach. In neither case should we force a meaning upon every detail. But the main outlines are always clear. In the symbolism of Scripture the connection between leprosy and sin is not doubtful." [1]

Anderson first quotes Leviticus 13:12-13 and then gives the truth which the type illustrates:

"If leprosy cover all the skin of him that hath the plague from his head even to his foot, wheresoever the priest looketh...he shall pronounce him clean that hath the plague" (Lev.xiii. 12,13).

"If we dissemble and cloak our sins, we need not look for mercy. Divine forgiveness is for sinners as such. 'Truth springeth out of the earth, and righteousness hath looked down from heaven' (Psalm 85:11, RV.) And the only truth which God requires from the sinner is the acknowledgment of what he is. 'Faithful is the saying, and worthy of all acceptation, that Christ Jesus came into the world to save sinners.' And with this confession of Christ must be joined the confession of sin and that must be in the spirit of the Apostle's words, 'of whom I am chief.' No false pleas based on supposed piety or penitence will avail; no pretence of being anything, or of having anything, to create a special claim for pardon. What God demands of us is truth - the

self-abasement of the full and unqualified acknowledgment of what we are." [2]

Anderson continues on this subject:

"Mark the words, 'the priest shall pronounce him clean that hath the plague.' He was to pronounce the 'leper' clean; and to pronounce him 'clean.' Not that he had not the plague, or that only a little of it showed; but if and when he was covered with disease from head to foot. The common belief is that Christ Jesus came into the world to save 'saints.' But the right word is 'sinners.' Pardon and salvation are for sinners. Not for sinners with a qualifying adjective, but for the ungodly, the guilty, and the lost. He came 'to seek and to save that which was lost.' " [3]

Anderson next points out another typical teaching and makes more comments on the typical teaching of Leviticus 13:12-13:

"The leper's habitation, we read, was 'outside the camp' ; and there, with rent clothes, bared head, and a covered lip, he was to cry, 'Unclean, unclean!' (Lev. xiii. 45.) The type thus teaches us the Divine estimate of sin...We have already noticed the striking ordinance that if the disease turned inwards the leper was unclean, but that he was to be pronounced clean if and when the leprosy was out over all his body. For sin cloaked or unconfessed there is nothing but banishment and wrath. But for the 'humble, lowly, penitent, and obedient' there is no reserve in Divine 'goodness and mercy.' " [4]

Next we will look at the actual ceremonial cleansing of the leper who was healed:

"Then shall the priest command to take for him that is to be cleansed two birds alive and clean, and cedar wood, and scarlet, and hyssop: And the priest shall command that one of the birds be killed in an earthen vessel over running water: As for the living bird, he shall take it, and the cedar wood, and the scarlet, and the hyssop, and shall dip them and the living bird in the blood of the bird that was killed over the running water: And he shall sprinkle

upon him that is to be cleansed from the leprosy seven times, and shall pronounce him clean, and shall let the living bird loose into the open field" (Lev.14:4-7).

In regard to this ritual Sir Robert remarks:

"One of the birds was to be killed, and its blood sprinkled on the leper. Death thus passed upon him; for such is always the meaning of blood-sprinkling." [5]

This teaches that remission of sins is impossible apart from shedding of blood:

"And almost all things are by the law purged with blood; and without shedding of blood is no remission" (Heb.9:22).

Anderson continues on the subject of the actual cleansing of the leper:

"The priest was then to take the live bird, and dipping it in the blood of the dead bird - thus identifying it with the dead bird - to let it loose as he uttered the word 'clean.' We now understand why two birds were needed to bring out all the truth. The Lord Jesus Christ 'was delivered for our offences, and was raised again for our justification' (Romans iv. 25.) ; and the release of the live bird was the public fact which proved to the leper that he was clean. The resurrection of Christ is the public proof that sin has been put away." [6]

We will now look at verses which contrasts a man who acknowledged his sinful condition with another man who did not:

"Two men went up into the temple to pray; the one a Pharisee, and the other a publican. The Pharisee stood and prayed thus with himself, God, I thank thee, that I am not as other men are, extortioners, unjust, adulterers, or even as this publican. I fast twice in the week, I give tithes of all that I possess. And the publican, standing afar off, would not lift up so much as his eyes unto heaven, but smote upon his breast, saying, God be merciful to me a sinner. I tell you, this man went down to his house justified ra-

ther than the other: for every one that exalteth himself shall be abased; and he that humbleth himself shall be exalted" (Lk.18:10-14).

The following is Anderson's commentary on these verses:

"A man who pleads his piety or his penitence is like a candidate for admission to an asylum for the pauper blind, who borrows good clothes to hide his poverty, and coloured spectacles to conceal his blindness. Such was the spirit of the Pharisee's plea. And every student of human nature, knows that the publican could have made out as plausible a case as the Pharisee. But he, taking his true place, cast himself unreservedly upon Divine mercy 'God, be merciful to me, a sinner' (Luke xviii. 13.). 'The sinner' was what he really said. England has three-score gaols full of prisoners; but in a criminal court the prisoner in the dock is 'the' prisoner. And such is the thought here such, the position of every one who really comes to the Cross." [7]

Notice that in the parable it was the one who acknowledged himself as being a sinner who *"went down to his house justified rather than the other."* That explains why Anderson says that the blessing is for the "self-judged and guilty":

"To weigh the evidences and embrace Christianity, as the true religion, is the part of a fair and prudent man; but salvation is God's work altogether. The blessing is not for the apt scholar, but for the outcast and lost. It is not for the clear head, but for the contrite heart. Not for the clever reasoner, but for the self-judged and guilty, not for logicians, but for sinners; not for the wise and prudent, but for babes." [8]

NOTES

1. Sir Robert Anderson, *Redemption Truths*, 61.

2. *Ibid.,* 62-63.

3. *Ibid.,* 64-65.

4. *Ibid.,* 64.

5. *Ibid.,* 65.

6. *Ibid.*

7. *Ibid.,* 63-64.

8. Sir Robert Anderson, *The Gospel And Its Ministry,* 52.

Chapter 11

Prophecy and Mystery

"Study to shew thyself approved unto God, a workman that needeth not to be ashamed, rightly dividing the word of truth" (2 Tim.2:15).

We are told to rightly divide the word of truth and one of the most important "divisions" within the Bible is the difference between the things relating to "prophecy" and the things which were kept "secret." Of course "prophecy" refers to the things which were foretold by the prophets while in the Bible the word "mystery" is used to denote things which were kept secret. Sir Robert says:

"Our English word 'mystery' means something which is either incomprehensible or unknown; but this is not the significance of the Greek 'musterion.' In its primary meaning in classical and Biblical Greek it is simply a secret; and a secret when once disclosed may be understood by any one...The mysteries of the New Testament are Divine truths which till then had been 'kept in silence'; truths which had not been revealed in the earlier Scriptures, and which, until revealed, could not be known." [1]

Anderson stresses the importance of recognizing the "mystery" truths, writing that if we ignore these truths then all sense of unity in the Bible will be lost:

"...thus ignoring the great 'mystery' truths revealed in the Epistles, the whole scheme of the Biblical revelation is dislocated, all sense of its Divine unity is lost, and faith in its Divine authority is undermined." [2]

He calls the present "dispensation of grace" the "Christian dispensation" and says it is a "New Testament mystery":

"This 'Christian Dispensation' is a New Testament 'mystery,' unknown to the people of God, and unnoticed in the Word of God, until after Israel had been set aside, and the Apostle to the Gentiles had received his call." [3]

Anderson also refers to the present dispensation as being an "intercalary" dispensation:

"When Israel was cast aside the clock of prophetic time was stopped, to be set in motion once again at the close of this intercalary 'Christian dispensation.' And then the Lord's prophetic words shall be fulfilled as though this age of ours had never intervened." [4]

The present dispensation is often called a "parenthetical" dispensation but things in a "parenthesis" can have some direct or indirect relationship to that which precedes or follows it. However, the things of the present dispensation are so divergent from God's purpose toward Israel that it can properly be called an "intercalation" because it is totally unrelated to the divine purpose relating to Israel. Sir Robert recognizes this fact:

"This Christian dispensation differs as essentially from the future as it does from the past." [5]

In order to see that the present dispensation is completely divorced from the prophesied program for Israel all we have to do is to look at the way that Gentiles are to be saved according to "prophecy." Here we see that Gentile salvation will be accomplished through the agency of Israel:

"In those days it shall come to pass, that ten men shall take hold out of all languages of the nations, even shall take hold of the skirt of him that is a Jew, saying, We will go with you: for we have heard that God is with you" (Zech.8:23).

According to prophecy when the Gentiles come to the knowledge of the Lord it will be through Israel:

"Surely you will summon nations you know not, and nations that do not know you will hasten to you, because of the Lord your God, the Holy One of Israel, for he has endowed you with splendor" (Isa.55:3,5; NIV).

"I will make an everlasting covenant with them. And their seed shall be known among the Gentiles, and their offspring among the people: all that see them shall acknowledge them, that they are the seed which the LORD hath blessed" (Isa.61:8-9).

In the present dispensation the Gentiles are not being saved by the agency of Israel but instead their salvation is through Israel's fall:

"I say then, Have they stumbled that they should fall? God forbid: but rather through their fall salvation is come unto the Gentiles, for to provoke them to jealousy. Now if the fall of them be the riches of the world, and the diminishing of them the riches of the Gentiles; how much more their fulness?" (Ro.11:11-12).

Anderson says the following in regard to Gentile salvation:

"Blessing for Gentiles is not a New Testament truth. It was assured by the promise to Abraham, and explicitly foretold in Hebrew prophecy. But that 'the people of the covenant' should lose nationally the privileged position of earthly testimony is a New Testament 'mystery' (Romans xi. 25)...from Genesis to Malachi, there is nothing in Scripture to suggest that they would ever lose their privileged position as the people of God. Their being 'cast off' was a crisis unparalleled since the call of Abraham." [6]

Sir Robert next states the result of the fall of Israel:

"Thus deprived of their stewardship, they are relegated to the position of other men. And the purpose and effect of their fall are stated in the words, 'God hath concluded them all in unbelief that He might have mercy upon all' (Romans xi. 32) Thus it was that

the way was opened up for the revelation of the great 'mystery'
truth of grace enthroned." [7]

As mentioned previously, before Israel's fall that nation was
said to be "above all people":

"For thou art an holy people unto the LORD thy God: the
LORD thy God hath chosen thee to be a special people unto him-
self, above all people that are upon the face of the earth"
(Deut.7:6).

As a result of Israel's fall there is now no difference between
those of Israel and the rest of mankind. Anderson stresses this
truth:

"Christianity, as a system, assumes the fact that in a former
age the Jews enjoyed a peculiar place in blessing...But the Jews
have lost their vantage-ground through sin, and they now stand
upon the common level of ruined humanity. The Cross has broken
down 'the middle wall' which separated them from Gentiles. It has
leveled all distinctions. As to guilt 'there is no difference, for all
have sinned' ; as to mercy 'there is no difference, for the same
Lord over all is rich unto all that call on Him.' How then, if there
be no difference, can God give blessing on a principle which im-
plies that there is a difference? In a word, the fulfillment of the
promises to Judah is absolutely inconsistent with the distinctive
truths of the present dispensation." [8]

From all of this we can understand that the things in regard to
the present "dispensation of grace" are unrelated to God's prophe-
sised program for Israel. Sir Robert writes:

"All Messianic prophecy relating to earth runs in the channel
of Israel's national history and therefore, so to speak, the clock of
prophetic time is stopped while their national history is in abey-
ance. And secondly, that Israel's rejection during this Christian
dispensation is a New Testament 'mystery.' " [9]

Again Anderson speaks of the confusion that will result unless we recognize the "mystery" truths:

"But so long as Israel's national position is in abeyance, the stream of fulfillment is tided back; or to change the figure, the hands upon the dial of prophetic time are motionless. Without this clew to guide us in our study of them, the Scriptures appear to be full of confusion, if not of error." [10]

Sir Robert illustrates what the prophets saw and did not see in the following way:

"The prophet's glance into the future entirely overlooked these nineteen centuries of our era. As when mountain peaks stand out together on the horizon, seeming almost to touch, albeit a wide expanse of river and field and hill may lie between, so there loomed upon the prophet's vision these events of times now long gone by, and times still future. And with the New Testament in our hands, it would betray strange and willful ignorance if we doubted the deliberate design which has left this long interval of our Christian era a blank." [11]

In other words, the "wide expanse of river and field and hill," which are in the valley between two mountains, represent the present "mystery dispensation" – a dispensation which was not seen by the prophets because the near mountain blocked the prophets' view.

Now let us examine the remaining "mystery" truths so that we will not confuse the things which belong to the present dispensation with the things revealed in prophecy.

The Three Great Mysteries

Sir Robert recognizes the following three great mysteries which relate to the present "dispensation of grace":

"The divine scheme of prophecy relating to earth, as unfolded in the Old Testament, has definite reference to the covenant peo-

ple; and their rejection of Christ seemed to thwart its fulfillment. But the sins of men cannot thwart the purposes of God; and their apostasy led to the revelation of a wider purpose which had been 'kept secret since the world began'...That revelation contains three, distinctive 'mysteries,' namely, the Gospel of Grace; the Church, the Body of Christ; and that 'Coming' which will be the consummation of this dispensation of Grace and of the Body." [12]

The Gospel of Grace

Anderson says that the "gospel of grace" was at one time a *"mystery which was kept secret since the world began"*:

"Here are his (Paul's) words: 'Now to him that is able to stablish you according to my gospel, even (kai) the preaching of Jesus Christ, according to the revelation of a mystery which was kept secret since the world began, but now is made manifest, and by prophetic writings, according to the commandment of the everlasting God, made known to all the nations unto obedience of faith' (Romans xvi. 25-26)."

"I have rendered the first 'kai' in this sentence by 'even'; for it is certain that the Apostle did not mean to distinguish between the gospel of Christ and a gospel of his own! And 'the Scriptures of the prophets' is a mistranslation which reduces his words to an absurdity; for he is thus made to say that this 'mystery' gospel was kept secret in all the past, and yet that it was taught in Old Testament Scriptures. His actual words are prophetic writings, i.e. the inspired Epistles of the New Testament. For a prophet is 'one who, moved by the Spirit of God, declares what he has received by inspiration' (Grimm's Lexicon); and therefore 'prophetic writings' is equivalent to inspired writings, the element of foretelling the future being purely incidental. And there can be no doubt that the 'mystery' of our verse is what the Apostle calls elsewhere 'the mystery of the gospel' - the reign of grace, which is the great basal truth of the distinctly Christian revelation - a truth which was not, and obviously could not be, declared until the covenant people were set aside. For grace is as incompatible with 'covenant,' or special favor of any kind, as it is with works." [13]

The heart and soul of the "gospel of grace" is the "purpose" of the Lord Jesus' death upon the Cross and Anderson equates that gospel to the "word of reconciliation":

"Though 'Grace came by Jesus Christ,' it was veiled during His earthly ministry. But when sin reached its climax the only possible alternatives were 'the doom of Sodom or the mercy of the Gospel' - judgment unmixed, or grace unlimited. And grace prevailed. God committed all judgment to the Lord Jesus Christ, and He, the only Being in the universe who can judge a sinner, is now seated on the throne of God as a Saviour. It is not merely that there is grace for all who come to God through Him, but that grace is reigning. The divine moral government of the world is not in abeyance, but all judicial or punitive action against sin is deferred (2 Pet. ii. 9). The great amnesty has been proclaimed. God is not imputing unto men their trespasses, but beseeching them to come within the reconciliation (2 Cor. V. 19,20)." [14]

The Christian has been given the "ministry of reconciliation" to preach the "word of reconciliation." Sir Robert writes:

"This great truth of Reconciliation will be sought in vain in the Old Testament Scriptures...Sin not merely alienated man from God, it alienated God from man. A just and holy God could not but regard him as an enemy. But 'while we were enemies we were reconciled to God by the death of His Son.' And 'through our Lord Jesus Christ' they who believe 'have now received the reconciliation.' (Rom. v. 10,11)-- 'All things are of God who reconciled us to Himself through Christ, and gave unto us the ministry of the reconciliation, to wit, that God was in Christ reconciling the world unto Himself not reckoning unto them their trespasses, and having committed unto us the word of the reconciliation. We are ambassadors, therefore, on behalf of Christ,' the apostle adds, 'as though God were entreating by us, we beseech men on behalf of Christ, be ye reconciled to God ' (2 Cor. v. 18-20) -- an appeal to the sinner, not, as too commonly represented, to forgive his God, but to come within the unsought benefit which God in His infinite grace has accomplished. For (the apostle further

adds) '*Him who knew no sin He made to be sinon our behalf, that we might become the righteousness of God in Him.*' " [15]

Next Sir Robert goes into more detail on this subject:

"*In this Christian dispensation God is not imputing their sins to men. Were it otherwise the silence of Heaven would give place to the thunders of His judgments. Every question of judgment was either settled for ever at the Cross, or has been postponed to the day that is still to come: God 'knows how' 'to reserve the unjust to the day of judgment to be punished' (2 Pet. ii. 9), and the day of judgment is not yet.*" [16]

In the following verses Paul speaks of the principles of this "good news" and uses the words "*But now…has been made known*":

"*But now a righteousness from God, apart from law, has been made known, to which the Law and the Prophets testify. This righteousness from God comes through faith in Jesus Christ to all who believe. There is no difference, for all have sinned and fall short of the glory of God, and are justified freely by his grace through the redemption that came by Christ Jesus*" (Ro.3:21-24; NIV).

Although all the saved in every age have been saved by grace through faith it was not until Paul when that truth was openly revealed.

"*For by grace are ye saved through faith; and that not of yourselves: it is the gift of God: Not of works, lest any man should boast*" (Eph.2:8-9).

The Body of Christ

"*And he is the head of the body, the church: who is the beginning, the firstborn from the dead; that in all things he might have the preeminence*" (Col.1:18).

In regard to the triumph of redemption and its relationship to the Body of Christ Sir Robert states:

"The triumph of redemption will not be in restoring us to the place which Adam lost by sin, but in raising us to the perfectness of the new creation, of which the Lord from heaven is the head." [17]

The Body of Christ is referred to as the "mystery of Christ" and it was kept secret and not made known in other ages:

"Whereby, when ye read, ye may understand my knowledge in the mystery of Christ. Which in other ages was not made known unto the sons of men, as it is now revealed unto his holy apostles and prophets by the Spirit; That the Gentiles should be fellow-heirs, and of the same body, and partakers of his promise in Christ by the gospel" (Eph.3:4-6).

Anderson says no trace of this "mystery" can be found in the OT:

"Some people regard the Old Testament as entirely superseded by the New, forgetting that all Scripture is God-breathed and profitable. And others again regard the New as merely an unfolding of the Old, forgetting that it reveals distinctively Christian truths of which no trace can be found in the Hebrew Scriptures. And in this category is 'the mystery of Christ.' The Apostle's words could not be more explicit: 'By revelation He made known unto me the mystery which in other ages was not made known unto the sons of men' (Eph. iii. 3,5)." [18]

Anderson says that the "mystery of Christ" spoken of in these verses is the believer's union with Christ:

"The mystery that in the present dispensation believers are united to Christ in a special relationship as members of a body of which He Himself is the head." [19]

Anderson goes into more detail, saying that "the mystery of Christ" is in regard to the closest possible relationship with the Lord Jesus:

" 'The mystery which from all ages hath been hid in God' - namely, that sinners of earth are called to the highest glory of heaven in the closest possible relationship with Christ. The bridal relationship and glory of the heavenly election from the earthly people of the covenant might well seem the acme of everything to which redeemed humanity could ever rise; but this crowning 'mystery' of the Christian revelation speaks of a bond more intimate and a glory more transcendent. The figure of the Bride betokens the closest union, but absolute oneness is implied in the figure of the Body." [20]

Anderson says that no one can be in union with Him until first we have been one with Him in that death which justifies:

"We can have no part whatever in His life on earth until first we have been made one with Him in that death which justifies. But, once united to Him, we stand accepted in all the perfectness of everything He is, and of everything He has ever proved Himself to be. 'If any man be in Christ, he is a new creature: old things are passed away; behold, all things are become new.' The Only-begotten Son has not come down to patch up the ruined fabric of the old creation; but, closing its history for ever by His death, to bring the redeemed of earth into a new creation of which He, the Lord from heaven, is the Head." [21]

Even though the Lord is forming the Body of Christ now Sir Robert says that that Body will not have a corporate existence until later:

"The Body of Christ is a truth of practical import for the Christian, profoundly influencing his personal life on earth, and his relationships with his fellow Christians. But yet 'the Church which is His body' is not on earth, nor can it have a corporate existence until all the members are brought in, and the Divine purpose respecting it is accomplished. The parallel of the bridal

relationship of the heavenly election out of Israel may teach us a lesson here. For it is not until the future age of the Apocalyptic visions that the Bride is displayed, and her marriage takes place. In like manner the consummation and display of the Body relationship awaits the coming of the Lord. For in the Divine purpose it is entirely for the glory of our Lord and Saviour that these elect companies of the redeemed are given positions of special nearness; and therefore the element of 'display' has prominence." [22]

Anderson has the following to say about the purpose of the Body being "for the glory of our Lord and Saviour":

"In words as profoundly true as they are simple, the Westminster Divines have taught us that 'Man's chief end is to glorify God and to enjoy Him for ever.' And this end will be realized when the redeemed of earth shall stand in heavenly glory, the whole record of their past having been laid bare before Him who 'died for their sins according to the Scriptures.' And every attribute of God — not merely His grace and love, but His holiness and righteousness — will be so displayed and vindicated that the unfallen of heaven will unite with the redeemed of earth in ascriptions of eternal praise." [23]

Caught Up to Meet Him in the Air

Anderson next speaks of another mystery, the one which will bring the present dispensation to a close:

"It is one of the 'mysteries' of the faith that, at the coming of the Lord, His people then living on earth shall pass at once to glory, 'with death untasted and the grave unknown.' The corruptible shall put on incorruption, the mortal immortality. And 'then shall be brought to pass the saying that is written, Death is swallowed up in victory.'" [24]

Here are verses that are in regard to this mystery:

"Behold, I shew you a mystery; We shall not all sleep, but we shall all be changed, In a moment, in the twinkling of an eye, at

the last trump: for the trumpet shall sound, and the dead shall be raised incorruptible, and we shall be changed. For this corruptible must put on incorruption, and this mortal must put on immortality" (1 Cor.15:51-53).

Sir Robert connects the words of 1 Corinthians 15:51-53 to the "catching up" of the saints:

"All the wide world over, wherever His dead have been laid to rest, 'the trump of God' shall call them back to life, in 'spiritual bodies' like His own; and wherever living 'saints' are found, they 'will be changed, in a moment, in the twinkling of an eye,' and all shall be caught up together to meet Him in the air." [25]

Here are the verses to which Anderson makes reference:

"For the Lord himself shall descend from heaven with a shout, with the voice of the archangel, and with the trump of God: and the dead in Christ shall rise first: Then we which are alive and remain shall be caught up together with them in the clouds, to meet the Lord in the air: and so shall we ever be with the Lord" (1 Thess.4:16-17).

These verses are in regard to a "mystery" so they have nothing to do with "prophecy." This coming of the Lord Jesus refers exclusively to those living in the present "mystery" dispensation. Anderson says:

"Mark the Apostle's words, 'I show you a mystery'; and in the Epistles the word 'mystery' indicates some truth which had remained secret up to the time of the Apostles. Seeing then that the Lord's Coming in judgment was prophesied by 'Enoch, the seventh from Adam' (Jude 14, 15), it cannot be the 'mystery' of 1 Corinthians xv. Neither can His Coming as the Son of Man; for that also is an Old Testament truth; and it had prominence in the Lord's own ministry. Indeed, these several 'Comings' have practically nothing in common, save that they all relate to Christ." [26]

One Shall Be Taken and the Other Left

As Anderson said, the "Coming of the Son of Man" was according to prophecy so it is not in regard to His coming which is described as being a "mystery." In the following verses the Lord Jesus also foretold of the "coming of the Son of Man":

"But of that day and hour knoweth no man, no, not the angels of heaven, but my Father only. But as the days of Noah were, so shall also the coming of the Son of man be...Then shall two be in the field; the one shall be taken, and the other left. Two women shall be grinding at the mill; the one shall be taken, and the other left" (Mt.24:36-37,40-41).

Here at the coming of the Son of Man *"one shall be taken and the other left."* These words of the Lord Jesus were in answer to His disciples' question concerning what will happen at *"the end of the age"*:

"Tell us, they said, when will this happen, and what will be the sign of your coming and of the end of the age?" (Mt.24:3; NIV).

Earlier the Lord had spoken a parable where He spoke of a "harvest" which would occur at the "end of the age":

"He answered and said unto them, He that soweth the good seed is the Son of man; The field is the world; the good seed are the children of the kingdom; but the tares are the children of the wicked one; The enemy that sowed them is the devil; the harvest is the end of the age; and the reapers are the angels. As therefore the tares are gathered and burned in the fire; so shall it be in the end of this age. The Son of man shall send forth his angels, and they shall gather out of his kingdom all things that offend, and them which do iniquity; And shall cast them into a furnace of fire: there shall be wailing and gnashing of teeth. Then shall the righteous shine forth as the sun in the kingdom of their Father" (Mt.13:37-43).

So at the "end of the age" it will be the unrighteous who will be taken out of the world and the righteous who will remain. This is certainly not describing the event when Christians will be caught up in the air because then it will be the righteous who are taken and the unrighteous who are left behind. Anderson says the following about the previously quoted verses from the 13th chapter of Matthew:

"Certain passages testify that Christ will return to earth, and stand once more on that same Olivet on which His feet last rested ere He ascended to His Father (Zech. xiv. 4); and others tell us as plainly that He will come, not to earth, but to the air above us, and call His people up to meet Him and be with Him (I Thess. iv. 16, 17). These Scriptures again most clearly prove that it is His believing people who shall be 'caught up,' leaving the world to run its course to its destined doom; while other Scriptures as unequivocally teach that it is not His people but the wicked who are to be weeded out, leaving the righteous 'to shine forth in the kingdom of their Father' (Matt. xiii. 40-43)." [27]

This shows the importance of distinguishing the "mystery" truths, which belong exclusively to the present dispensation, from the things which relate to God's program for Israel, a program which is according to "prophecy." Anderson continues on this theme:

"Some of us have learned to distinguish between 'the coming of the Son of Man' in judgment, 'to gather out of His Kingdom all things that offend and them which do iniquity' (Matt. xiii. 41), and the coming of the Lord, as Saviour, to call His people out of earth to heaven." [28]

NOTES

1. Sir Robert Anderson, *The Silence of God*, 109.

2. Sir Robert Anderson, *Misunderstood Texts of the New Testament*, 26.

3. Sir Robert Anderson, *Forgotten Truths*, 75.

4. *Ibid.,* 73.

5. *Ibid.,* 37.

6. *Ibid.,* 15, 129.

7. *Ibid.,* 43.

8. Sir Robert Anderson, *The Coming Prince*, 152.

9. Sir Robert Anderson, *Misunderstood Texts of the New Testament*, 18.

10. Sir Robert Anderson, *Forgotten Truths*, 72-73.

11. Sir Robert Anderson, *The Coming Prince,* 46-47.

12. Sir Robert Anderson, *Types in Hebrews,* 170.

13. Sir Robert Anderson, *Misundersood Texts of the New Testament*, 82-83.

14. Sir Robert Anderson, *Types in Hebrews,* 171.

15. Sir Robert Anderson, *The Silence of God*, 112-114.

16. *Ibid.,* 141.

17. Sir Robert Anderson, *The Lord From Heaven*, 33.

18. Sir Robert Anderson, *Forgotten Truths*, 38-39.

19. Sir Robert Anderson, *The Silence of God*, 110.

20. Sir Robert Anderson, *Forgotten Truths*, 38.

21. Sir Robert Anderson, *The Gospel and Its Ministry*, 115.

22. *Ibid.,* 39.

23. *Ibid.,* 133.

24. Sir Robert Anderson, *Redemption Truths*, 166.

25. Sir Robert Anderson, *The Coming Prince,* 288.

26. Sir Robert Anderson, *Misunderstood Texts of the New Testament*, 90.

27. Sir Robert Anderson, *The Coming Prince*, 154-155.

28. Sir Robert Anderson, *Forgotten Truths*, 50.

Chapter 12

The Day of Pentecost and Miracles

The idea that the present "mystery" dispensation started on the day of Pentecost is believed by practically all Christians. However, we can see that the events of that time period were in relation to "prophecy" and not to something kept "secret."

On the day of Pentecost Peter addressed the following words to the nation of Israel:

"Repent ye therefore, and be converted, that your sins may be blotted out, when the times of refreshing shall come from the presence of the Lord. And he shall send Jesus Christ, which before was preached unto you: Whom the heaven must receive until the times of restitution of all things, which God hath spoken by the mouth of all his holy prophets since the world began" (Acts 3:19-21).

Anderson says that Peter's words about "the times of restitution of all things" were in regard to prophecy:

"As the inspired Apostle declared at Pentecost, 'the times of the restitution of all things' — or, in other words, the times when all things will be put right — are the burden of Hebrew prophecy from Moses to MalachI (Acts iii. 19), and the fulfillment of these prophecies awaits the return of Christ." [1]

Anderson also says the following about the same words of Peter:

"To represent this as Christian doctrine, or the institution of 'a new religion', is to betray ignorance alike of Judaism and of

Christianity. The speakers were Jews -the apostles of One who was Himself 'a minister of the circumcision'. Their hearers were Jews, and as Jews they were addressed. The Pentecostal Church which was based upon the testimony was intensely and altogether Jewish. It was not merely that the converts were Jews, and none but Jews, but that the idea of evangelising Gentiles never was even mooted. When the first great persecution scattered the disciples, and they 'went everywhere preaching the Word', they preached, we are expressly told, 'to none but to the Jews'."

"The Jerusalem Church, then, was Jewish. Their Bible was the Jewish Scriptures. The Jewish temple was their house of prayer and common meeting-place. Their beliefs and hopes and words and acts all marked them out as Jews...Nothing was further from the thoughts of these men than 'founding a new religion'. On the contrary, while hailing the rejected Nazarene as their national Messiah, they clung with passionate devotion to the religion of their fathers." ²

The Gift of the Holy Spirit

On the day of Pentecost believers began to speak in languages of which they had no knowledge and some people said that they were drunk (Acts 2:13). Then we read:

"But Peter, standing up with the eleven, lifted up his voice, and said unto them, Ye men of Judaea, and all ye that dwell at Jerusalem, be this known unto you, and hearken to my words: For these are not drunken, as ye suppose, seeing it is but the third hour of the day. But this is that which was spoken by the prophet Joel; And it shall come to pass in the last days, saith God, I will pour out of my Spirit upon all flesh: and your sons and your daughters shall prophesy, and your young men shall see visions, and your old men shall dream dreams" (Acts 2:14-17).

What was happening was a fulfillment of what the prophet Joel had foretold hundreds of years earlier:

"And it shall come to pass afterward, that I will pour out my spirit upon all flesh; and your sons and your daughters shall prophesy, your old men shall dream dreams, your young men shall see visions: And also upon the servants and upon the hand-maids in those days will I pour out my spirit" (Joel 2:28-29).

This prophecy was the subject of the Lord Jesus' words spoken to His Apostles after He was resurrected but before He ascended into heaven:

"On one occasion, while he was eating with them, he gave them this command: Do not leave Jerusalem, but wait for the gift my Father promised, which you have heard me speak about. For John baptized with water, but in a few days you will be baptized with the Holy Spirit" (Acts 1:4-5; NIV).

From this we can understand that the "gift" which was promised by the Father was in regard to being "baptized with the Holy Spirit." Here Peter speaks of that "gift":

"Peter replied, Repent and be baptized, every one of you, in the name of Jesus Christ for the forgiveness of your sins. And you will receive the gift of the Holy Spirit" (Acts 2:38).

Does this mean that the gift is the Holy Spirit or does this speak of a gift that is bestowed by the Holy Spirit? Let us look at the following verse that speaks of multiple gifts that were bestowed by the Holy Spirit:

"God also bearing them witness, both with signs and wonders, and with divers miracles, and gifts of the Holy Spirit, according to his own will?" (Heb.2:4).

From this we can understand that the Holy Spirit bestowed multiple gifts of one kind or another to some believers. At Acts 2:38 the reference is just to one gift. It is not difficult to understand exactly what "gift" of the Spirit was received on that day. In the following verses we can see that the "gift" that was bestowed by the Holy Spirit on the day of Pentecost was the ability to speak in tongues:

"When the day of Pentecost came, they were all together in one place. Suddenly a sound like the blowing of a violent wind came from heaven and filled the whole house where they were sitting. They saw what seemed to be tongues of fire that separated and came to rest on each of them. All of them were filled with the Holy Spirit and began to speak in other tongues as the Spirit enabled them" (Acts 2:1-4; NIV).

It was the Holy Spirit which enabled the believers to speak in other tongues. This "gift" is among the same gifts which Paul refers to in the following verses:

"Now there are diversities of gifts, but the same Spirit...For to one is given by the Spirit the word of wisdom...to another divers kinds of tongues; to another the interpretation of tongues" (1 Cor.12:4,8-10).

Those who submitted to the rite of water baptism on the day of Pentecost received a gift bestowed by the Holy Spirit--the ability to speak in tongues. Sir Robert next points out that the miracles were chiefly in regard to the Lord Jesus' ministry to the Jews:

"The gospel of Christ was not 'the beginning of the oracles of God'; it was another chapter in a long-continued revelation. But it had a two-fold aspect. He came to a people whose every hope, for earth and heaven centred in a Messiah promised to their fathers, and He came, moreover, to a world that was ruined and lost. His mission, therefore, had a two-fold character and purpose. He was the Messiah to the Jew; He was the bread of God to give life to the world. It was with the former that the miracles had specially to do." [3]

Anderson says that the miracles had specifically to do with the Lord Jesus' ministry to the Jew. Sir Robert continues on this subject:

"So long as the gospel was being proclaimed especially to the covenant people, miracles abounded. For it was primarily to the covenant people that Christ came. 'Salvation is of the Jews,' the Lord declared. 'I am not sent, but to the lost sheep of the house of Israel.' 'Christ was a minister of the circumcision, for the truth of God, to confirm the promises made unto the fathers' (Romans xv. 8). That ministry, therefore, had special reference to the Scriptures which testified of Him and which it was His mission to fulfill." [4]

Let us look at what Anderson says about the Abrahamic race and miracles:

"The history of the Abrahamic race, to which prophecy is so closely related, is little else than a record of miraculous interpositions." [5]

Anderson then quotes Fynes Clinton:

" 'Their passage out of Egypt was miraculous. Their entrance into the promised land was miraculous. Their prosperous and their adverse fortunes in that land, their servitudes and their deliverances, their conquests and their captivities, were all miraculous. The entire history from the call of Abraham to the building of the sacred temple was a series of miracles. It is so much the object of the sacred historians to describe these that little else is recorded' (Clinton, 'Fasti H.', vol. i, p.243)." [6]

With the advent of Christ the miracles resumed. Let us go back to the beginning of the ministry of the Lord Jesus when He preached in the synagogue of Nazareth and quoted from the book of Isaiah:

"And he came to Nazareth, where he had been brought up: and, as his custom was, he went into the synagogue on the sabbath day, and stood up for to read. And there was delivered unto him the book of the prophet Esaias. And when he had opened the book, he found the place where it was written, The Spirit of the Lord is upon me, because he hath anointed me to preach the gos-

pel to the poor; he hath sent me to heal the brokenhearted, to preach deliverance to the captives, and recovering of sight to the blind, to set at liberty them that are bruised, To preach the acceptable year of the Lord" (Lk.4:16-19).

The Lord Jesus was quoting the following prophecy from the Old Testament which revealed that Israel's Messiah would heal the blind:

"The Spirit of the Lord is upon me, because he has anointed me; he has sent me to preach glad tidings to the poor, to heal the broken in heart, to proclaim liberty to the captives, and recovery of sight to the blind; to declare the acceptable year of the Lord" (Isa.61:1-2: Lancelot C. L. Brenton, English translation of the *LXX*, The Greek version of the OT).

Sir Robert says that the Lord's miracles were of the type which the Jews expected from their Messiah:

"It was not merely that they were miracles, but that they were such miracles as the Jews were led by their Scriptures to expect. Their significance depended on their special character, and their relation to a preceding revelation accepted as Divine by those for whose benefit they were accomplished." [7]

The miracles were especially for those who had a knowledge of the Old Testament prophecies so therefore the miracles were given to the Jews in order to provide proof to them that the Lord Jesus is the promised Messiah. Anderson continues:

"When the Nazarene appeared, the question with the Jew was not whether, like another John the Baptist, He was 'a man sent of God,' but whether He was the Sent One, the Messiah to whom all their religion pointed and all their Scriptures bore testimony. 'We have found the Messiah': 'We have found Him of whom Moses in the law, and the prophets, did write' (John i. 41,45). Such were the words in which His disciples gave expression to their faith, and by which they sought to draw others to Him. The question, then, is not whether a revelation can be accredited by external

evidence, but whether such evidence can avail to accredit a person whose coming has been foretold. And this no accurate thinker would for a moment dispute." [8]

The purpose of the miracles was to accredit the Lord Jesus as Messiah and the evidence that He is the Messiah was contained in the Old Testament prophecies. Therefore the miracles were chiefly for those who possessed the Old Testament Scriptures. The Lord Jesus said the following about His "works," or things which He did in during His ministry:

"But I have greater witness than that of John: for the works which the Father hath given me to finish, the same works that I do, bear witness of me, that the Father hath sent me" (Jn.5:36).

The Lord Jesus said that the works which He did bore "witness" of Him. In regard to the miracles Anderson says:

"It is nowhere suggested that they were given to accredit the teaching; their evidential purpose was solely and altogether to accredit the Teacher." [9]

To support this view, Anderson says the following:

"There had never risen a greater prophet than John the Baptist; and yet at the very time this testimony was given to him, his 'political' faith, if I may use the expression, had broken down, and his disciples were on their way back to his prison, to reassure him by the record of the Lord's miracles." [10]

Here is an account of the events of which Anderson speaks:

"Now when John had heard in the prison the works of Christ, he sent two of his disciples, And said unto him, Art thou he that should come, or do we look for another? Jesus answered and said unto them, Go and shew John again those things which ye do hear and see: The blind receive their sight, and the lame walk, the lepers are cleansed, and the deaf hear, the dead are raised up, and the poor have the gospel preached to them" (Mt.11:2-5).

Earlier it was pointed out that Anderson said the testimony which was to the Jews was of a "twofold" nature:

"The testimony had a twofold accompaniment. 'The Sermon on the Mount' is recorded as embodying the great truths and principles which were associated with the Kingdom Gospel; and the attendant miracles gave proof that all was Divine." [11]

When He sent His Apostles to preach the gospel of the kingdom miracles followed. Sir Robert says that this ministry was limited to the Jew:

"In the earlier stages of the ministry of Christ, His miracles were not reserved for those whose faith responded to His words; the only qualification for the benefit was that the recipient should belong to the favored race. 'Go not into the way of the Gentiles, and into any city of the Samaritans enter ye not: but go rather to the lost sheep of the house of Israel. And as ye go, preach, saying, The kingdom of heaven is at hand. Heal the sick, cleanse the lepers, raise the dead, cast out devils: freely ye have received, freely give.' Such was the commission under which the twelve went forth through that little land, to every corner of which their Master's fame had gone before them. (Matt. iv. 24,25)." [12]

Anderson sums up his argument concerning miracles in the following way:

"The miracles were not given as a bait to attract the unbeliever but as a beacon to guide the seeker after truth. Their purpose was to prove 'that Jesus was the Christ'; therefore they were intended especially for those who had the preceding revelation, for those who had the Scriptures which foretold His coming. They were the sign for those who knew the countersign." [13]

Anderson says that when the special testimony to the Jews ceased then the "purpose" of the miracles was accomplished:

"...the special testimony to the Jews having ceased, the purpose for which miracles were given was accomplished." [14]

This special testimony ceased at the end of the period of time covered by the book of *Acts*. Sir Robert next gives evidence that the miracles ceased after that period of time:

"It is matter, not of opinion but of fact, that whereas Pentecostal gifts and evidential miracles hold a prominent place in the narrative of the Acts and in the teaching of Epistles written during the period historically covered by the Acts, the later Epistles are silent with respect to them. The natural inference is that the miracles and gifts had ceased, and the Epistles of the apostle Paul's last imprisonment give proof that this inference is right. 'In nothing am I behind the very chiefest apostles,' he declared, when appealing to the 'signs and wonders and mighty deeds' which were the outward credentials of his ministry (2 Corinthians xii. 11-12). For 'God wrought special miracles by the hands of Paul,' so that even handkerchiefs carried from his body brought healing to the sick (Acts xix. 11-12). Why then was it that he could not heal Epaphroditus when he lay 'sick nigh unto death' by his side at Rome? How was it that, at a still later date, he had to leave Trophimus lying sick at Miletum (Philippians ii. 27; 2 Timothy iv. 20)?" [15]

By the time when the period of time covered by the Acts record had ceased Paul was unable to heal either Epaphroditus or Trophimus. Nonetheless today there are some who claim to be able to heal with the power of the Holy Spirit.

"Spirits" Which Are Not of God

The Scriptures of the New Testament give warnings about "spirits" which are not of God:

"Now the Spirit speaketh expressly, that in the latter times some shall depart from the faith, giving heed to seducing spirits, and doctrines of devils" (1 Tim.4:1).

"Beloved, believe not every spirit, but try the spirits whether they are of God: because many false prophets are gone out into the world" (1 Jn.4:1).

Anderson speaks of those who are deceived by signs and wonders at the present time:

"In the ages before Christ came, men may well have craved for public proofs of the action of a personal God. But in the ministry and death and resurrection of the Lord Jesus Christ, God has so plainly manifested, not only His power, but His goodness and love-toward-man, that to grant evidential miracles, now, would be an acknowledgment that questions which have been for ever settled are still open. Moreover, miracles of another kind abound. For in recent years the gospel has achieved triumphs in heathendom, which transcend anything recorded in the Acts of the Apostles. And infidelity is thus confronted by surer proofs of the presence and power of God than any miracle in the natural sphere could offer. For miracles in the natural sphere are not necessarily a proof of Divine action: they are the lure by which some of the demon cults of the present day ensnare their dupes; and the time may be near when such signs and wonders will abound." [16]

Anderson continues, saying that seeking out spirit manifestations *"smacks of unbelief and not faith and may lead to disaster"*:

"A Christian is not one who has certain feelings or experiences, nor even one who believes in the Holy Ghost; he is a believer in the Lord Jesus Christ. It is the Word of the truth of the gospel which brings us the knowledge of Christ. Men once saw Him with their eyes and their hands handled Him; but ours is the blessedness of those who have not seen and yet have believed. For He is now 'within the veil' (Hebrews 6:19), and if our anchor is 'both sure and stedfast,' it is because it 'entereth into that which is within the veil.' God's written Word is our only cable. The craving to get 'within the veil' by means of spiritual gifts and manifestations smacks of unbelief and not of faith, and may lead to disaster. Let us take earnest heed to the solemn warning spoken by the Lord:

"Many will say to Me in that day, 'Lord, Lord, have we not prophesied in Thy Name? and in Thy name have cast out devils?

and in Thy Name done many wonderful works?' And then will I profess unto them, 'I never knew you; depart from Me, ye that work iniquity' " (Matthew 7:22-23). " [17]

Certainly the Lord Jesus was referring to the "unsaved" since He said that He never knew them. Despite this they were able to make prophecies and "cast out devils" and do "wonderful works" so it is evident that the source of these miracles is not God.

NOTES

1. Sir Robert Anderson, *Forgotten Truths*, 5.

2. Sir Robert Anderson, *The Silence of God*, 75-78.

3. Sir Robert Anderson, *The Gospel And Its Ministry*, 203-204.

4. Sir Robert Anderson, *Spirit Manifestations and the Gift of Tongues* (Windber, PA: Bible Student's Press, 2009), 11.

5. Sir Robert Anderson, *The Coming Prince,* 165-166.

6. *Ibid.,* 166.

7. Sir Robert Anderson, *The Silence of God*, 41.

8. *Ibid.,* 45.

9. *Ibid.,* 41.

10. Sir Robert Anderson, *The Gospel And Its Ministry*, 50.

11. Sir Robert Anderson, *The Coming Prince,* 160.

12. *Ibid.*

13. Sir Robert Anderson, *Spirit Manifestations and the Gift of Tongues*, 11.

14. Sir Robert Anderson, *The Silence of God*, 58.

15. Sir Robert Anderson, *Spirit Manifestations and the Gift of Tongues*, 12.

16. Sir Robert Anderson, *Forgotten Truths*, 31.

17. Sir Robert Anderson, *Spirit Manifestations and the Gift of Tongues*, 14.

Chapter 13

The Satan Myth

Anderson points out that the idea that Satan is responsible for the sins of mankind is nothing but a myth and therefore his real influence is not evident to most people:

"THE devil of Christendom is a myth. Just as human fancy, working on a basis of fact and truth, has impersonated an object for its worship, so by a like process it has created a scapegoat to account for the crimes and vices of humanity...The Satan of Christian mythology is a monster of wickedness, the instigator to every crime of exceptional brutality or loathsome lust." [1]

Anderson says that it is not in the realm of morals where Satan has his greatest sway:

"How it would simplify matters if morality were a distinctive badge of the regenerate, and immorality characterised the rest! But vice is not the hall-mark of the devil's handiwork. 'A form of godliness' (2 Tim. iii. 5) is one of his 'devices.' Among the most dangerous enemies of Christ and Christianity, are men who live pure and upright lives, and who preach righteousness. 'And no marvel; for even Satan fashioneth himself into an angel of light: It is no great thing therefore if his ministers also fashion themselves as ministers of righteousness' (2 Cor. xi. 14,15). And if 'the very elect' are deceived by the fraud, it is mainly because they are blinded by this error of the Satan myth." [2]

The god of This World

"But if our gospel be hid, it is hid to them that are lost: In whom the god of this world hath blinded the minds of them which believe not, lest the light of the glorious gospel of Christ, who is the image of God, should shine unto them" (2 Cor.4:3-4).

Sir Robert says that the words "god of this world" in the preceding verses are referring to Satan:

"The god of this world" is his awful title - a title Divinely conceded to the Evil One, not because the Supreme has delegated His sovereignty, but because the world accords him its homage. It is in the sphere of religion, then, that the influence of the Tempter is to be sought - not in the records of our criminal courts, not in the pages of obscene novels, but in the teaching of false theologies." [3]

Satan's speciality is the teaching of false theologies, and he does that by controlling false religions:

"And no marvel; for Satan himself is transformed into an angel of light. Therefore it is no great thing if his ministers also be transformed as the ministers of righteousness; whose end shall be according to their works" (2 Cor.11:14-15).

Sir Robert states that it is the religions of the world which Satan controls:

"According to Holy Writ, he 'fashions himself into an angel of light,' and 'his ministers fashion themselves as ministers of righteousness.' Do 'ministers of righteousness' corrupt men's morals or incite them to commit outrages?...It is the religion of the world that he controls, and not its vices and its crimes...Hence it is that men turn to the Church, to religion, to morality, to 'the Sermon on the Mount' - making the Lord Himself minister to their self-righteousness and pride - in a word, to anything and everything rather than to the Cross of Christ." [4]

Today, through the influence of Satan, the foundational truths of Christianity are rejected by many. Anderson says:

"The mind of the Tempter is disclosed no less in some of our most popular books of piety. Eternal judgment and a hell for the impenitent, redemption by blood, and the need of salvation through the death of the great Sin-bearer - these and kindred doctrines are rejected as survivals of a dark and credulous age: it is for man to work out his own destiny, and to raise himself to the Divine ideal. And all this is prefaced and made plausible by boldly insinuating that plain words Divinely spoken are either misunderstood or spurious. A new gospel some men call this: it is the oldest gospel known. In every point it reminds us of the old, old words: 'Hath God said?' 'Ye shall not surely die': 'Ye shall be as gods knowing good and evil.' The 'Jesus' of this theology bears a sinister resemblance to the great philanthropist of Eden!" [5]

The following verses demonstrate that Satan's goal was to undermine the faith of Peter:

"And the Lord said, Simon, Simon, behold, Satan hath desired to have you, that he may sift you as wheat: But I have prayed for thee, that thy faith fail not: and when thou art converted, strengthen thy brethren" (Lk.22:31-32).

The Lord Jesus prayed that Peter's "faith fail not." In his commentary on these verses Anderson says:

"When Satan asked to have Peter (as he had asked to have Job) it was his faith he sought to destroy. 'I made supplication for thee,' the Lord added, 'that thy faith fail not.' And with the memory of this before him no doubt it was that the apostle wrote the words, 'Your adversary the devil, as a roaring lion, walketh about, seeking whom he may devour: whom withstand stedfast in your faith' (1 Pet v. 8-9)." [6]

Anderson continues on this theme, writing that Satan is the enemy of faith:

"In the parable of the tares in the field, it is the devil who sows the tares (Matt. xiii. 39). And in the parable of the sower the devil's work is described as taking away the word out of the

hearts of those who hear it, 'lest they should believe and be saved'
(Lk. viii. 12). And if Elymas the sorcerer was called a 'son of the
devil,' it was because of his 'seeking to turn aside the proconsul
from the faith' (Acts xiii. 8, 10)...In Rev. xii. 9 (R.V.), he is called
"the deceiver of the whole world" (cf Rev. xx. 10); and in that
book he is represented as the leader in the great coming struggle
between faith and unfaith, between the acknowledgment of God
and the denial of Him...In his 'devices' upon men the Satan of
Scripture is the enemy, not of morals, but of faith." [7]

Next we will look at the following verses which detail the only way that a believer can deal effectively with Satan:

"Put on the whole armour of God, that ye may be able to
stand against the wiles of the devil. For we wrestle not against
flesh and blood, but against principalities, against powers,
against the rulers of the darkness of this world, against spiritual
wickedness in high places....take the helmet of salvation, and the
sword of the Spirit, which is the word of God" (Eph.6:11-12,17).

In order to stand against the wiles of the devil we must put on
the whole armour of God, including "the word of God." Sir Robert says:

"The old classification of 'the world, the flesh, and the devil' is
a right one. And 'our wrestling is not against flesh and blood.' In
the 'flesh' sphere our safety is in flight. But flight from Satan is
impossible. 'Flee youthful lusts' (2 Tim. ii. 22); but 'Resist the
devil, and he will flee from you' (James iv. 7). Such is the distinc-
tion clearly marked in Scripture. The baser 'lusts of the flesh' are
entirely under a man's control, unless indeed he is enervated by
vicious indulgence; but with the strongest and holiest of men 'the
whole armour of God' is the only sure defence against the attacks
of Satan." [8]

Anderson says that the goal of Satan is to lead us away from
the doctrines revealed in the Holy Scriptures:

"Of the devil's aim and methods I have already spoken. No one, I repeat, may assert that he might not use the basest means to ensnare a minister of Christ, and thus mar his testimony and destroy his usefulness. But it cannot be asserted too often or too plainly that his normal effort is not to tempt to the commission of sins such as lead to contrition, and teach us how weak we are; but, by drawing us away to mere human morality, or religion, or philosophy, to deaden or destroy our sense of dependence upon God. For sin may humble a Christian; but human philosophy and religion can only foster his self-esteem. And pride is 'the snare of the devil' (1 Tim. iii. 6,7); not humility." [9]

Here Sir Robert is more specific about the target of the "god of this world":

"Satan is the god of this world, and therefore the religion of the world is the normal sphere of his activities. And, as Luther said, all his assaults are aimed at Christ Himself. He blinds the minds of men to the revelation of a Christ who is 'the image of God' (2 Cor. iv. 4-6). The Deity of Christ is thus his main objective, for upon that depends everything that is vital in Christianity. Hence his campaign against the Bible. For no one whose mind is not warped or blinded by the superstitions of religion can fail to recognize that it is only through the written Word that we can reach 'the living Word.'" [10]

NOTES

1. Sir Robert Anderson, *The Silence of God*, 117.

2. *Ibid.,* 192-193.

3. *Ibid.,* 127.

4. *Ibid.,* 126-128.

5. *Ibid.,* 128-129.

6. *Ibid.,* 183.

7. *Ibid.,* 183-184.

8. *Ibid.,* 194-195.

9. *Ibid.,* 195.

10. Sir Robert Anderson, *Forgotten Truths*, 101-102.

Chapter 14

The Deity of Christ

Sir Robert writes that the Deity of Christ is the foundation truth of Christianity:

"If...we let go the Deity of Christ, which is the foundation truth of Christianity, the doctrine of the Atonement is destroyed. For in the whole range of false religions there is not a more grotesquely silly superstition than that the death of a fellow-creature could expiate the sin of the world." [1]

Anderson stresses the importance of the truth that the Lord Jesus is God:

"Everything depends upon the Deity of Christ; and, therefore, as Athanasius said long ago, in contending for that great truth 'we are contending for our all.' " [2]

The Son of God

The Lord Jesus referred to Himself as the "Son of God." According to the following verses we can understand what meaning the Jews placed on that title. When the Jews threatened to stone the Lord Jesus He said to them:

" 'I have shown you many good works from the Father. For which of these do you stone me?' 'We are not stoning you for any good work,' they replied, 'but for blasphemy, because you, a mere man, claim to be God.' " (Jn.10:32-33; NIV).

The Jews sought to kill Him because they understood Him to be claiming to be God. They got that understanding because the

Lord applied the title "Son of God" to Himself, as witnessed by His words to them in reply:

"Say ye of him, whom the Father hath sanctified, and sent into the world, Thou blasphemest; because I said, I am the Son of God?" (Jn.10:36).

We can see that when the Lord Jesus said that God was His Father the Jews understood Him to be claiming to be God:

"But Jesus answered them, My Father worketh hitherto, and I work. Therefore the Jews sought the more to kill him, because he not only had broken the sabbath, but said also that God was his Father, making himself equal with God" (Jn.5:17-18).

The Lord Jesus was charged with blasphemy because He claimed to be God and it for this reason that the Jewish leaders sought His death:

"When the chief priests therefore and officers saw him, they cried out, saying, Crucify him, crucify him. Pilate saith unto them, Take ye him, and crucify him: for I find no fault in him. The Jews answered him, We have a law, and by our law he ought to die, because he made himself the Son of God" (Jn.19:6-7).

Anderson says that it was because the Lord Jesus called Himself the Son of God that the Jews sought the death penalty:

"We must remember that the Jews were not a tribe of ignorant savages, but a highly cultured and intensely religious people; and it was upon this very charge that, without a dissentient voice, His death was decreed by the Sanhedrim - their great national Council, composed of the most eminent of their religious leaders, including men of the type of Gamaliel and his great pupil, Saul of Tarsus. That He was of the royal house of David was proved by the official genealogies. That He did great miracles was universally acknowledged, and not even His enemies denied that all His acts and, save on one vital point, all His words, were Worthy of His Messianic claims. How, then, can the fact be accounted for

that good men - men who had a zeal for God- condemned Him to death as a blasphemer? The answer is not doubtful. It was not for His good deeds that He had been threatened with stoning, but because, said they, 'Thou, being a man, makest Thyself God.' And upon this charge it was, I repeat, that He was arraigned. Had that charge been false, had it been due to a perversion of His words, He would, as a devout Jew, have repudiated it with indignant earnestness, whereas His acceptance of it was unequivocal." [3]

The Son of Man

A look at the following statement addressed to Elymas will help us understand one of the meanings of the term *"Son of..."* in the Scriptures:

"You who are full of all deceit and fraud, you son of the devil, you enemy of all righteousness, will you not cease to make crooked the straight ways of the Lord?" (Acts 13:10; NASB).

Sir Robert says that the expression "son of…" refers to a person's character and nature:

"When the Apostle Paul denounced Elymas the sorcerer as 'Thou son of the devil,' his Oriental hearers would understand his words as describing the man's character and nature." [4]

Then Anderson speaks about how the title "Son of Man" applied to the Lord Jesus:

"It was not His human birth that constituted Him the Son of Man. That birth, indeed, was the fulfillment of the promise which the name implied; but the Son of Man, He declared explicitly, 'descended out of heaven.' And He said again, 'What and if ye shall see the Son of Man ascend up where He was before?' When, therefore, He proclaims that 'the Son of Man came to seek and to save that which was lost,' came 'to give His life a ransom for many,' faith responds intelligently in the words of that noblest of the Church's hymns, 'When Thou tookest upon Thee to deliver

*man, Thou didst not abhor the Virgin's womb.' For the Virgin
birth was but a stage in the fulfilment of His mission."* [5]

With this in mind we can more clearly understand how "man"
can be said to be created in the image of God. Anderson says:

*"The revelation of the Son of Man will lead the spiritual
Christian, who has learned to note the hidden harmony of Scripture, to recall the language of the creation story: 'Let us make
man in our image, after our likeness.' 'The type,' as the biologist
would phrase it, is not the creature of Eden, but He after whose
likeness the creature was fashioned."* [6]

The Only Begotten

The following is one of the most quoted verses of those who
deny the Deity of Christ:

*"And the Word was made flesh, and dwelt among us, (and we
beheld his glory, the glory as of the only begotten of the Father),
full of grace and truth"* (Jn.1:14).

Those who deny that the Lord Jesus is God say that this verses
demonstrates that He was begotten by the Father so therefore He
is a creature just like we are. To answer this Sir Robert says:

*"As the Lord's title of Son of Man does not mean that He was
begotten by a man, but that He is the very impersonation of humanity, ought we not to interpret His title of Son of God on this
same principle? But is He not called the 'only begotten Son of
God'? Such is indeed the inaccurate rendering of our English
versions. Etymologically 'only begotten,' as one word, would be
the precise equivalent in English of the Greek word here used;
but what concerns us is not the etymology of the word, but the
meaning of it. The language of the New Testament is largely
based upon that of the Greek version of the Old; and this word is
used by the LXX. to represent a Hebrew term of endearment - a
term in which there is no suggestion whatever of 'begetting.' It*

properly denotes 'only'; and by a natural transition it comes to mean 'unique,' and then 'greatly beloved.' " [7]

From the following verse we can understand that the word "begotten" as it applies to the Lord Jesus has nothing to do with His birth at Bethlehem but instead refers to His resurrection from the dead:

"God hath fulfilled the same unto us their children, in that he hath raised up Jesus again; as it is also written in the second psalm, Thou art my Son, this day have I begotten thee" (Acts 13:33).

The word "begotten" here refers to the resurrection and not to the birth of the Lord Jesus. The Greek word translated "only begotten" is *monogenes*, and it is used in the following verse which speaks of Isaac:

"By faith Abraham, when he was tried, offered up Isaac: and he that had received the promises offered up his only begotten (monogenes) son" (Heb.11:17).

In regard to the phrase "only begotten" Anderson says that:

"Our translators regarded this English phrase as a term of endearment; for Isaac, though his father's darling, was not his only son." [8]

The Son as the Firstborn

In the following verse the Lord Jesus is called "the firstborn":

"The Son is the image of the invisible God, the firstborn (prototokos) over all creation" (Col.1:15; NIV).

The word "firstborn" is translated from the Greek word *prototokos*, and that same word is also used in the following verse:

"To the general assembly and church of the firstborn (pro-totokos), which are written in heaven, and to God the Judge of all, and to the spirits of just men made perfect" (Heb.12:23).

Sir Robert says that the word has a figurative or spiritual meaning:

"In its ordinary use 'prototokos' means a woman's first child, being a male. But Hebrews 12:23 gives proof that it acquired a figurative or spiritual significance, suggested by, and wholly apart from, its common meaning. For every individual in the particular company of the redeemed there designated is a 'firstborn,' and it is clearly used as a title of special dignity and privilege. This being so, it would be ignorant and wrong to narrow its application to our Divine Lord by reference to the virgin birth, or to construe it as implying in any way a limitation of His Deity...In the sphere of creation the term 'firstborn' can be applied to the Lord only as a title of dignity and glory. And this is presumably its significance in those passages also which relate to the resurrection." [9]

What the Disciples Believed

Anderson says that the Lord Jesus' disciples worshipped Him as divine:

"If, then, His title of Son of God does not depend on the Virgin birth - and it is a fact of vital moment that the word 'begotten' is used of Him only in relation to His resurrection from the dead - what can be its significance? The only meaning that can be given to it is that which it conveyed to those who heard His teaching, those among whom He lived and died. Just as by 'Son of Man' He claimed to be man in the highest and most absolute sense, so by 'Son of God' He laid claim to Deity. His disciples understood it thus, and they worshipped Him as divine; and those who refused to believe in Him understood it thus, and they crucified Him as a blasphemer." [10]

His disciples did in fact worship their Lord and Savior as "God," as witnessed by the following exchange between the Lord Jesus and Thomas:

"Then saith he to Thomas, Reach hither thy finger, and behold my hands; and reach hither thy hand, and thrust it into my side: and be not faithless, but believing. And Thomas answered and said unto him, My LORD and my God. Jesus saith unto him, Thomas, because thou hast seen me, thou hast believed: blessed are they that have not seen, and yet have believed" (Jn.20:27-29).

The Lord Jesus did not rebuke Thomas for calling Him God which would have been expected of any devout Jew who was called God but yet was not God. Instead, the Lord Jesus pronounced a blessing on all who come to faith without seeing His visible and resurrected body. Here the Apostle John speaks of that blessing:

"And many other signs truly did Jesus in the presence of his disciples, which are not written in this book: But these are written, that ye might believe that Jesus is the Christ, the Son of God; and that believing ye might have life through his name" (Jn.20:30-31).

All Things Were Made By Him

The following verses refer to the Lord Jesus as the "Word" and say that "the Word was God" and that "all things were made by Him":

"In the beginning was the Word, and the Word was with God, and the Word was God. The same was in the beginning with God. All things were made by him; and without him was not any thing made that was made" (Jn,1:1-3).

Commenting on these verses Sir Robert says:

"We are told, 'All things were made by Him'; and if the Creator of all things be not God, language has no meaning." [11]

154

The Apostle Paul affirms that the Lord Jesus made all things:

"The Son is the image of the invisible God, the firstborn over all creation. For in him all things were created: things in heaven and on earth, visible and invisible, whether thrones or powers or rulers or authorities; all things have been created through him and for him. He is before all things, and in him all things hold together" (Col.1:15-17; NIV).

NOTES

1. Sir Robert Anderson, *The Lord From Heaven*, 14.

2. *Ibid.*, 15.

3. *Ibid.*, 22.

4. *Ibid.*, 28.

5. *Ibid.*, 30-31.

6. *Ibid.*, 31-32.

7. *Ibid.*, 40.

8. *Ibid.*, 41.

9. *Ibid.*, 109.

10. *Ibid.*, 45-46.

11. *Ibid.*, 11.

Chapter 15

Justification by Works

Let us look again at the verses which say that Satan blinds the minds of those who do not believe the gospel:

"But even if our gospel is veiled, it is veiled to those who are perishing, whose minds the god of this age has blinded, who do not believe, lest the light of the gospel of the glory of Christ, who is the image of God, should shine on them" (2 Cor.4:3-4; NKJV).

Sir Robert explains the meaning of the words "gospel of the glory of Christ" here:

" 'Show me Thy glory, I beseech Thee,' was the prayer of Moses; and God answered, 'I will make all My goodness pass before thee, and I will proclaim the name of Jehovah before thee, and will be gracious to whom I will be gracious, and will show mercy on whom I will show mercy.' God's highest glory displays itself in sovereign grace, therefore it is that the gospel of His grace is the gospel of His glory." [1]

The "gospel of the glory of Christ" is the "gospel of His grace." How does Satan blind people's minds to the truth of the gospel of grace? First let look closely at the "gospel of grace." The Apostle Paul says that the believer is "justified freely":

"...justified freely by His grace through the redemption that is in Christ Jesus" (Ro.3:24).

One of the meanings of the Greek word translated "freely" is *"without just cause."* [2]

The same word is used in the following verse in regard to the Jew's treatment of the Lord Jesus:

"*They hated Me without a cause*" (Jn.15:25).

The believer is justified before God "without a cause". If "works" were required for salvation then the Lord would have a "cause" for justifying a sinner. But Paul makes it plain that the believer is justified "without cause." That is why Paul can say that the reward comes "*to him that worketh not, but believeth*":

"*Now to him that worketh is the reward not reckoned of grace, but of debt. But to him that worketh not, but believeth on him that justifieth the ungodly, his faith is counted for righteousness*" (Ro.4:4-5).

Paul explains that if works are required then the reward cannot be said to be according to the principle of "grace." To make it even more plain he writes that the reward comes to those who "worketh not" but "believeth." The religions which Satan controls teach that before a man can be "right" with God that he must be worthy by his "works" or "deeds." However, the Scriptures declare that eternal life is a "gift":

"*For the wages of sin is death; but the gift of God is eternal life through Jesus Christ our Lord*" (Ro.6:23).

Satan's master stroke to undermine the principle of "salvation by grace" is his teaching that both "faith" and "works" are required in order to receive this gift of eternal life. Here is a verse which he quotes in order to accomplish his goal:

"*Was not Abraham our father justified by works, when he had offered Isaac his son upon the altar? Seest thou how faith wrought with his works, and by works was faith made perfect?*" (James.2:21-22).

Sir Robert quotes these verses and then says:

"Justification by works, as an article of man's religion, is opposed to justification by faith, and therefore it denies the grace of God, and dishonours the blood of Christ." [3]

How do we explain the fact that James includes "works" when he speaks of justification even though in the following verse Paul denies that "works" has anything to do with a man's justification before God?:

"But to him that worketh not, but believeth on him that justifieth the ungodly, his faith is counted for righteousness" (Ro.4:5).

Anderson says that first we must examine the very nature of the two epistles where these seemingly contradictory ideas are found:

"The Epistle to the Romans is essentially doctrinal, and the practical is based upon the doctrine. The Epistle 'to the twelve tribes scattered abroad,' is essentially practical, the doctrinal element being purely incidental. Paul's Epistle unfolds the mind and purposes of God, revealing His righteousness and wrath. The Epistle of James addresses men upon their own ground. The one deals with justification as between the sinner and God, the other as between man and man." [4]

Sir Robert says that the book of James "addresses men upon their own ground." Indeed, we can see that the epistle of James is dealing with what one person may know about another person's faith, as evidenced by the following words from the pen of James:

"Even so faith, if it hath not works, is dead, being alone. Yea, a man may say, Thou hast faith, and I have works: shew me thy faith without thy works, and I will shew thee my faith by my works" (James 2:17-18).

James says, *"Show me your faith without works and I will show you my faith by my works."* This is obviously in regard to what people can know about other people's faith. Now let us look at the following verse:

"What doth it profit, my brethren, though a man say he hath faith, and have not works?" (James 2:14).

Anderson says that these words also demonstrate that the matter is in regard to what a man can know about other men's faith:

" 'What is the profit if a man say he hath faith, and have not works?' Not 'If a man have faith,' but 'If a man 'say' he hath faith' ; proving that, in the case supposed, the individual is not dealing with God, but arguing the matter with his brethren. God, who searches the heart, does not need to judge by works, which are but the outward manifestation of faith within; but man. can judge only by appearances." [5]

Next, Sir Robert goes into more detail on this subject:

"Faith identifies a sinner with a Saviour God. But it is nothing in itself. A man cannot show another his faith, any more than he can show him his charity. One who says he has faith, but whose conduct is not that of a believer, is like a man who says he has charity, but does no charitable actions ; who dismisses a starving beggar with kind words and nothing more." [6]

With that in mind let us look at these verses from the epistle of James:

"Even so faith, if it hath not works, is dead, being alone...Thou believest that there is one God; thou doest well: the devils also believe, and tremble" (James 2:17,19).

With these verses Anderson sums up his argument:

" 'Even so,' says the Epistle. just in the same sense, 'faith, if it hath not works, is dead, being alone.' You believe in one God. Well, quite right so do the devils ; and what comes of it? They tremble, and so ought you. Believing cannot, therefore, be in itself a meritorious thing. But if it be indeed, to use a favourite metaphor, a laying hold of God, it will declare itself by results. Abraham's case is an instance. He believed God, and it was imputed unto him for righteousness. That is, Abraham believed and God

blessed him, 'He was holden for righteous, in virtue of faith.'
Well, the result was that Abraham acted. God discerned the faith;
man judged of the acts. He believed, and God declared he was
righteous. He acted, and man acknowledged he was righteous. He
was justified by faith when judged by God, for God knows the
heart. He was justified by works when judged by his fellow-men;
for man can only read the life. And just as faith is made perfect,
or fulfilled, by works, so the Scripture which says 'He was justi-
fied by faith,' is made perfect, or fulfilled, by the declaration, 'He
was justified by works.' So then, though in one sense a man is jus-
tified by faith without works, in another sense we see 'how by
works a man is justified, and not by faith only.' Justified by faith
before God ; justified by works before men." [7]

Therefore we can understand that one reference to "justification" is in regard to men and the other to God. Therefore it is no
coincidence when we read that Paul himself made the same distinction:

"For if Abraham were justified by works, he hath whereof to
glory; but not before God" (Ro.4:2).

"But not before God"!

NOTES

1. Sir Robert Anderson, *The Gospel And Its Ministry*, 9.

2. Joseph Henry Thayer, *A Greek-English Lexicon of the New Testament*, 161.

3. Sir Robert Anderson, *The Gospel And Its Ministry*, 159.

4. *Ibid.*, 160.

5. *Ibid.*

6. *Ibid.*

7. *Ibid.*, 161.

Chapter 16

The Judgment Seat of Christ

"Wherefore also we make it our aim, whether at home or absent, to be well-pleasing unto him. For we must all be made manifest before the judgment-seat of Christ; that each one may receive the things done in the body, according to what he hath done, whether it be good or bad" (2 Cor.5:9-10; ASV).

There are many Bible teachers who say that every Christian will be judged at the "judgment-seat of Christ" as to whether or not he or she will be saved. However, Anderson says:

"Upon two main points the teaching of Scripture is explicit; the consequences of accepting or rejecting Christ are eternal; and the destiny of all will be declared by the resurrection. For the resurrection will be either 'unto life' or unto judgment; and the saved will be raised in bodies 'fashioned like unto His glorious body.' And it is as thus; 'raised in glory' that we shall be judged." [1]

The Christian will be raised in glory when he meets the Lord Jesus in the air and puts on a glorious body just like the Lord's glorious body:

"But our citizenship is in heaven. And we eagerly await a Savior from there, the Lord Jesus Christ, who, by the power that enables him to bring everything under his control, will transform our lowly bodies so that they will be like his glorious body" (Phil.3:20-21; NIV).

The following words of the Apostle Paul describes exactly what will be judged in that day:

"According to the grace of God which is given unto me, as a wise masterbuilder, I have laid the foundation, and another buildeth thereon. But let every man take heed how he buildeth there upon...Every man's work shall be made manifest: for the day shall declare it, because it shall be revealed by fire; and the fire shall try every man's work of what sort it is. If any man's work abide which he hath built thereupon, he shall receive a reward. If any man's work shall be burned, he shall suffer loss: but he himself shall be saved; yet so as by fire" (1 Cor.3:10,13-15).

In his commentary on these verses Sir Robert says:

"No less definite, however, is the statement that in that day one 'shall receive a reward,' while another 'shall suffer loss.' 'Yes,' someone will say, 'but that relates to service.' Precisely so. And this principle, perhaps, underlies the whole judgment of the redeemed. Only let us avoid the error which so soon corrupted the early Church, of separating off the 'religious' from the 'secular' element in Christian life. In all his relationships, and in the discharge of all his duties in life, the Christian is the servant of God, and as a servant he shall give account of himself to God." [2]

At 1 Corinthians 3:15 Paul says that even though a Christian's "work" in service may be burned *"he himself shall be saved."* Next, Anderson comments on the context where the phrase *"judgment-seat of Christ"* is used:

"For 'the judgment-seat of Christ' is not the dread tribunal of 'the great white throne' of the Patmos vision. The 'we' of the tenth verse is the 'we' of all the verses that precede and follow it. The whole passage breathes confidence and courage. God has 'wrought' us for immortality, and He has given us the Holy Spirit as the earnest of that which is our assured destiny." [3]

Here are verses which precede the words "judgment-seat of Christ":

"For we know that if our earthly house of this tabernacle were dissolved, we have a building of God, an house not made with hands, eternal in the heavens. For in this we groan, earnestly desiring to be clothed upon with our house which is from heaven: If so be that being clothed we shall not be found naked. For we that are in this tabernacle do groan, being burdened: not for that we would be unclothed, but clothed upon, that mortality might be swallowed up of life. Now he that hath wrought us for the selfsame thing is God, who also hath given unto us the earnest of the Spirit" (2 Cor.5:1-8).

Anderson says that these verses are speaking about our natural bodies as well as the bodies we will put on when we meet the Lord Jesus in the air:

"Our 'natural body' is likened to the tabernacle, the 'spiritual body' to a building - not, like the temple, built on earth by human hands, but a building of God, eternal, and in the heavens. Then the symbolism changes. Death is likened to our being unclothed, 'found naked' ; and our receiving our heavenly body without passing through death is symbolized by our being 'clothed upon'-- the change which the Coming of the Lord will bring to those 'who are alive and remain' when mortality shall he swallowed up of life. And our longing is for this (v. 2)." [4]

The "change which the Coming of the Lord will bring" to believers is described here:

"Behold, I shew you a mystery; We shall not all sleep, but we shall all be changed, In a moment, in the twinkling of an eye, at the last trump: for the trumpet shall sound, and the dead shall be raised incorruptible, and we shall be changed. For this corruptible must put on incorruption, and this mortal must put on immortality" (1 Cor.15:51-53).

By the time of the judgment-seat of Christ believers will have already received immortal, incorruptible bodies. With this in mind let us look at the verse under discussion again:

"For we must all be made manifest before the judgment-seat of Christ; that each one may receive the things done in the body, according to what he hath done, whether it be good or bad" (2 Cor.5:10; ASV).

The primary meaning of the Greek word translated "bad" in this verse is "worthless." Anderson says:

"The forensic tone given to the passage by the word 'judgment-seat' may be foreign to its intention. This suggestion is greatly strengthened by the Revised Text, where 'bad' is displaced by 'phaulos' - one of those words, as Archbishop Trench notices, 'which contemplate evil under another aspect, that, namely, of its good-for-nothingness.' And, he adds, 'This notion of worthlessness is the central notion of phaulos,' though the word runs through other meanings until it reaches 'bad'; 'but still bad predominantly in the sense of worthless.' " [5]

Therefore when the Christian will be judged for his service he will be rewarded for any work which the Lord judges to be good while his works which are deemed "worthless" will be burned, *"but he himself shall be saved."*

The Christian will be judged in regard to His service for God but he will not be judged in regard to salvation, as witnessed by the following words of the Lord Jesus:

"Verily, verily, I say unto you, He that heareth my word, and believeth him that sent me, hath eternal life, and cometh not into judgment, but hath passed out of death into life" (Jn.5:24; ASV).

Sir Robert addresses these words, writing that

"The believer in the Lord Jesus Christ 'cometh not into judgment, but hath passed out of death into life.' He has forgiveness of sins here and now. And he is not only forgiven, but justified. And he has peace with God; and instead of looking forward to the day of wrath, he is called to 'rejoice in hope of the glory of God' (Rom. v. 1-2)." [6]

NOTES

1. Sir Robert Anderson, *Forgotten Truths*, 118.

2. Sir Robert Anderson, *Redemption Truths*, 147.

3. Sir Robert Anderson, *Forgotten Truths*, 117.

4. Sir Robert Anderson, *Misunderstood Texts of the New Testament*, 94.

5. Sir Robert Anderson, *Forgotten Truths*, 118-119.

6. Sir Robert Anderson, *Redemption Truths*, 142-143.

Chapter 17

The Blessed Hope

"Looking for that blessed hope, and the glorious appearing of the great God and our Saviour Jesus Christ" (Titus 2:13).

The Christian will put on a new, glorious body just like the Lord Jesus' body when he meets Him in the air, and this is called the *"blessed hope."* Anderson writes:

"For the believer in Christ...the salvation of the soul is a present blessing, yet, 'as a creature,' the Christian still groans under the ruin. 'Even we ourselves groan within ourselves, waiting for our adoption, to wit, the redemption of our body.' This is 'salvation by hope.' But the hope is far removed from doubt. For God has promised, and the work is His. The redeemed sinner is 'foreordained to be conformed to the image of His Son." [1]

As Anderson says, this "hope" is far removed from doubt because God has promised. In fact, it is "foreordained" that the redeemed of the present dispensation will be *"conformed to the image of His Son"*:

"For whom he did foreknow, he also did predestinate (proorizo) to be conformed to the image of his Son, that he might be the firstborn among many brethren" (Ro.8:29).

Predestination

Anderson explains the significance of the Greek word which is translated "predestinate" in the following way:

"The word 'proorizo,' on which theology has reared such an imposing edifice, occurs only in the four following passages: Acts 4:28 ; Romans 8:29, 30; 1 Corinthians 11:7; and Ephesians 1: 5, 11. In two only of these, moreover, is it used with reference to the destiny of men; and never in relation to life, but only to special positions of blessing to which the redeemed are predestinated. In our present verse it is 'to be conformed to the image of His Son.' And in keeping with this, in Ephesians 1:5 we are said to be predestinated 'unto adoption as sons.' " [2]

Most Bible teachers say that when the word "predestinate" is used in regard to a man's destiny it is speaking of the idea that some men are foreordained to be saved while others are not. However, Sir Robert says that when the word "predestinate" is used in regard to a man's destiny it is never used in regard to salvation but instead only to a "special position of blessing" for those who are already saved or redeemed.

The Christian will be *"conformed to the image of His Son"* when He meets Him in the air and puts on a glorious body just like His glorious body:

"But our citizenship is in heaven. And we eagerly await a Savior from there, the Lord Jesus Christ, who, by the power that enables him to bring everything under his control, will transform our lowly bodies so that they will be like his glorious body" (Phil.3:20-21; NIV).

The same Greek word translated "predestinate" is also used in regard to the "adoption":

"Having predestined us to adoption as sons by Jesus Christ to Himself, according to the good pleasure of His will" (Eph.1:5; NKJV).

That is the same "adoption" that is regard to the redemption of the body:

"And not only they, but ourselves also, which have the firstfruits of the Spirit, even we ourselves groan within ourselves, waiting for the adoption, to wit, the redemption of our body" (Ro.8:23).

It is foreordained that all of the redeemed of the present dispensation will meet the Lord in the air and at that time they will put on bodies which are described as being immortal:

"Behold, I shew you a mystery; We shall not all sleep, but we shall be changed...For this corruptible must put on incorruption, and this mortal must put on immortality" (1 Cor.15:51,53).

Sealed Unto the Day of Redemption

The body which is described as being "incorruptible" in the previous verses is also referred to as the Christian's "inheritance":

"To an inheritance incorruptible, and undefiled, and that fadeth not away, reserved in heaven for you" (1 Pet.1:4).

This inheritance is also foreordained or predestinated:

"In whom also we have obtained an inheritance, being predestinated according to the purpose of him who worketh all things after the counsel of his own will" (Eph.1:11).

Just a few verses later Paul speaks of this same inheritance:

"In whom ye also trusted, after that ye heard the word of truth, the gospel of your salvation: in whom also after that ye believed, ye were sealed with that Holy Spirit of promise, Which is the earnest of our inheritance until the redemption of the purchased possession" (Eph.1:13-14).

Once the sinner believes he is sealed with the Holy Spirit and the Holy Spirit is the earnest of his inheritance until the redemption of the purchased possession. Later in the same epistle Paul says:

"And grieve not the holy Spirit of God, whereby ye are sealed unto the day of redemption" (Eph.4:30).

The Christian has been sealed with the Holy Spirit and he will remain sealed until the day of redemption. The "day of redemption" is described in the following verse which was quoted earlier:

"And not only they, but ourselves also, which have the firstfruits of the Spirit, even we ourselves groan within ourselves, waiting for the adoption, to wit, the redemption of our body" (Ro.8:23).

At Ephesians 1:14 Paul referred to the Holy Spirit being *"the earnest of our inheritance until the redemption of the purchased possession"* and at another place he speaks of that same "earnest" in the context of the Christian being "clothed upon" with an immortal body:

"For we that are in this tabernacle do groan, being burdened: not for that we would be unclothed, but clothed upon, that mortality might be swallowed up of life. Now he that hath wrought us for the selfsame thing is God, who also hath given unto us the earnest of the Spirit" (2 Cor.5:5).

These verses first speak of when the Christian will put on an "immortal body" and then ties the "earnest of the Spirit" to that destiny. Anderson says that God has given us the Holy Spirit as the earnest of our destiny:

"God has 'wrought' us for immortality, and He has given us the Holy Spirit as the earnest of that which is our assured destiny." [3]

The Scriptures reveal that immediately after believing the Christian has been given the Holy Spirit as the "earnest" of the purchased possession, the new glorious body which he will receive when he is caught up to meet the Lord Jesus in the air. The "earnest" is a down payment with a guarantee of more to come.

The following verse speaks of the "seal" which Christians have received:

"Nevertheless, the foundation of God standeth sure, having this seal, The Lord knoweth them that are his" (2 Tim.2:19).

All those who have believed belong to God, having been purchased by the ransom being paid:

"Even as the Son of man came not to be ministered unto, but to minister, and to give his life a ransom for many" (Mt.20:28).

A very high price has been paid for the redemption of lost sinners and that price is the precious blood of the Lord Jesus:

"Forasmuch as ye know that ye were not redeemed with corruptible things, like silver and gold...but with the precious blood of Christ, as a lamb without blemish and without spot" (1 Pet.1:18-19).

That is the same "price" to which Paul makes reference here:

"Know ye not that your body is the temple of the Holy Spirit who is in you, whom ye have of God, and ye are not your own? For ye are bought with a price; therefore, glorify God in your body and in your spirit, which are God's" (1 Cor.6:19-20).

The Christian belongs to God and he is not his own. Sir Robert affirms this fact:

"By the death of Christ, the believer is released from every claim and penalty pertaining to his former state. He is redeemed, bought back by God, and is, now, absolutely God's." [4]

A very steep price has been paid to redeem those who believe and God will not allow any of His possessions to be separated from Him. Sir Robert quotes Romans 8:35-39, verses which speak of God's love for those who belong to Him:

"What, then, shall we say to these things? If God be for us, who can be against us? He that spared not His own Son, but delivered Him up for us all, how shall He not with Him also freely give us all things? Who shall lay anything to the charge of God's elect? It is God that justifieth. Who is He that condemneth? It is Christ that died, yea, rather, that is risen again, Who is even at the right hand of God, Who also maketh intercession for us. Who shall separate us from the love of Christ? Shall tribulation, or distress, or persecution, or famine, or nakedness, or peril, or sword? As it is written, For Thy sake we are killed all the day long; we are accounted as sheep for the slaughter. Nay, in all these things we are more than conquerors through Him that loved us. For I am persuaded, that neither death, nor life, nor angels, nor principalities, nor powers, nor things present, nor things to come, nor height, nor depth, nor any other creature, shall be able to separate us from the love of God, which is in Christ Jesus our Lord." [5]

The Scriptures reveal that God has foreordained that all who believe during the present dispensation will put on new, glorious bodies just like the Lord Jesus' glorious body. Not only that, but at the very moment when the sinner believes he is given the Holy Spirit as the earnest of this promise of a glorious body and that earnest serves as God's guarantee or pledge of the fulfillment of that promise.

When the Christian meets the Lord Jesus in the air he will put on the promised glorious body and from that moment on *"shall ever be with the Lord"*:

"For the Lord himself shall descend from heaven with a shout, with the voice of the archangel, and with the trump of God: and the dead in Christ shall rise first: Then we which are alive and remain shall be caught up together with them in the clouds, to meet the Lord in the air: and so shall we ever be with the Lord" (1 Thess.4:16-17).

Then Paul adds:

"Wherefore comfort one another with these words."

Heavenly Bodies

Anderson says that the "coming of the Lord Jesus" when Christians will be caught up to meet the Him in the air is:

"the Coming of the Lord Jesus Christ to take His people home from earth to heaven. 'For the Lord Himself shall descend from heaven with a shout, with the voice of the archangel, and with the trump of God; and the dead in Christ shall rise first; then we which are alive and remain, shall be caught up together with them in the clouds, to meet the Lord in the air; and so shall we ever be with the Lord.' (1 Thess. iv. 16,17)." [6]

Christians will be caught up to meet the Lord Jesus in the air and they will be taken to heaven. At this time the Christians who remain alive will be "changed," putting on spiritual bodies just like those of the resurrected saints who will precede them:

"So also is the resurrection of the dead. It is sown in corruption; it is raised in incorruption...it is sown a natural body; it is raised a spiritual body" (1 Cor.15:42,44).

Here the Apostle Paul compares the different bodies spoken of in the Scriptures:

"For we know that if our earthly house of this tabernacle were dissolved, we have a building of God, an house not made with hands, eternal in the heavens. For in this we groan, earnestly desiring to be clothed upon with our house which is from heaven: If so be that being clothed we shall not be found naked. For we that are in this tabernacle do groan, being burdened: not for that we would be unclothed, but clothed upon, that mortality might be swallowed up of life" (2 Cor.5:1-4).

On these verses Sir Robert says:

"The symbolism of the 5th chapter is as simple as it is graphic. Our 'natural body' is likened to a tent, the spiritual body to a

house. Not a house like the Jerusalem temple, built on earth by human hands, and liable to perish; but a building of God, eternal, and in the heavens. Then the symbolism assumes another phase. Death is likened to our being unclothed; and in contrast with being thus stripped naked, our receiving the heavenly body without passing through death is symbolized by our being 'clothed upon.' Three distinct conditions are thus indicated — clothed, clothed upon, and found naked. The first is our condition during our life on earth, and the last is that to which death reduces us. This is plain to all; but the 'being clothed upon' is apt to be misunderstood. It does not refer to the Resurrection, but to the change which the Coming of the Lord will bring to those 'who are alive and remain.' " [7]

From this we can understand that the spiritual body which the Christian will put on when he is caught up to meet the Lord Jesus in the air will be a body "which is from heaven." And that is exactly what Peter is referring to when he says that it is "reserved in heaven":

"Blessed be the God and Father of our Lord Jesus Christ, which according to his abundant mercy hath begotten us again unto a living hope by the resurrection of Jesus Christ from the dead, To an inheritance incorruptible, and undefiled, and that fadeth not away, reserved in heaven for you" (1 Pet.1:3-4).

It is the same heavenly body that Paul refers to here as being a "hope" which is *"laid up for you that is in heaven"*:

"We give thanks to God and the Father of our Lord Jesus Christ, praying always for you, Since we heard of your faith in Christ Jesus, and of the love which ye have to all the saints, For the hope which is laid up for you in heaven, whereof ye heard before in the word of the truth of the gospel" (Col.1:3-5).

The destination of the Christian when he will be caught up is "heaven," referred to in the following verses as the "kingdom of God":

"And as we have borne the image of the earthy, we shall also bear the image of the heavenly. Now this I say, brethren, that flesh and blood cannot inherit the kingdom of God; neither doth corruption inherit incorruption. Behold, I shew you a mystery; We shall not all sleep, but we shall all be changed" (1 Cor.15:49-51).

In a commentary written by the Dallas Theological Seminary faculty David K. Lowery writes that men in their flesh and blood bodies cannot enter the eternal kingdom:

"With all that had preceded about the need for the natural body to give way to the spiritul, it followed that 'flesh and blood,' the natural body, could not eneter the eternal state." [8]

Anderson says that the Lord Jesus is now in heaven but not in a flesh and blood body:

" 'Flesh and blood' are not essential to humanity. True it is that, as 'the children are partakers of flesh and blood, He also Himself likewise took part of the same' (Heb. ii. 14). He assumed 'a natural body.' 'For there is a natural body, and there is a spiritual body.' The one pertains to 'the first man,' who is 'of the earth earthy,' the other to 'the second Man,' who is 'of heaven.' For the Lord from heaven is 'Very Man,' and it is as Man that He is now upon the throne. But the body is not the man: it is but the tent, the outward dress, as it were, which covers Him. And He is 'the same yesterday, and to-day, and for ever' (Heb. xiii. 8); the same who once trod the roads of Galilee and the streets of Jerusalem. He is enthroned as Man, but no longer now in 'flesh and blood.' For ere He 'passed through the heavens' He changed His dress." [9]

The Imminent Appearing of the Lord Jesus Christ

Let us look at the following verse which is in regard to the time when the Christian will be caught up in the air:

"And not only they, but ourselves also, which have the firstfruits of the Spirit, even we ourselves groan within ourselves, waiting for the adoption, to wit, the redemption of our body" (Ro.8:23).

Here Paul speaks of "waiting" for the "redemption of our body." Just a few verses earlier Paul speaks of the Christian expecting the "revealing" of the sons of God:

" "For I reckon that the sufferings of this present time are not worthy to be compared with the glory which shall be revealed to us-ward. For the earnest expectation of the creation waiteth for the revealing of the sons of God" (Ro.8:18-19; ASV).

Anderson says that these verses are speaking of "the deliverance of the creature" that remains in the future:

"The deliverance of the creature is still future. For while the sinner receives the reconciliation when he believes in Christ, 'the earnest expectation of the creation waiteth for the revealing of the sons of God.' " [10]

The Greek word translated "earnest expectation" is *apokaradokia*, and this word means:

"to watch with head erect or outstretched...to wait for in suspense." [11]

Sir Robert says that the Greek word translated "earnest expectation" expresses the thought of something believed to be imminent:

"the strongest that any language could supply to express the earnest expectation of something believed to be imminent. According to Bloomfield, 'it signifies properly to thrust forward the head and neck as in anxious expectation of hearing or seeing something.'...Such, then, is the Divinely-chosen word, to indicate what ought to be our attitude toward the return of Christ. And it is a kindred word that the Apostle uses in his Epistle to Titus, dated probably in the very year of his martyrdom, where he tells us

that the training of the school of grace leads us to live 'looking for that blessed hope' (Titus ii. 12, 18). As Dean Alford says: 'The Apostolic age maintained that which ought to be the attitude of all ages, constant expectation of the Lord's return.' " [12]

The Apostle Paul teaches that the Lord could return at any moment so therefore he would not be telling anyone to be thrusting forward their head in an expectation of the Lord Jesus' return if certain events must first precede His return. Sir Robert speaks of this "constant expectation" of the return of the Lord Jesus and its relationship to His return as revealed in the 24th chapter of Matthew:

"Most strange it is that any Christian who studies the 24th chapter of Matthew can tolerate the thought that the Lord would tell us to live looking for His Coming, if intervening events barred the fulfillment of His words. For here in His teaching about His Coming as Son of Man, He warns His earthly people to look, not for His Coming, but for 'things that must come to pass' before His Coming. And His words, 'Watch, for ye know not what hour your Lord doth come,' relate to a time when every intervening event has actually come to pass, and not a line of prophecy has to be fulfilled before His return." [13]

NOTES

1. Sir Robert Anderson, *Redemption Truths*, 158-159.

2. Sir Robert Anderson, *Misunderstood Texts of the New Testament*, 76-77.

3. Sir Robert Anderson, *Forgotten Truths*, 117.

4. Sir Robert Anderson, *The Gospel and Its Ministry*, 113.

5. Sir Robert Anderson, *Redemption Truths*, 159-160.

6. Sir Robert Anderson, *Forgotten Truths*, 45.

7. *Ibid.,* 62-63.

8. John Walvoord and Roy Zuck, *The Bible Knowledge Commentary; New Testament* [Colorado Springs: ChariotVictor Publishing, 1983], 545.

9. Sir Robert Anderson, *The Lord From Heaven,* 32.

10. Sir Robert Anderson, *Redemption Truths*, 163.

11. Joseph Henry Thayer, *A Greek-English Lexicon of the New Testament*, 62.

12. Sir Robert Anderson, *Misunderstood Texts of the New Testament*, 92.

13. Sir Robert Anderson, *Forgotten Truths*, 79-80.

Chapter 18

The Preaching of the Cross

"For the preaching of the cross is to them that perish foolishness; but unto us which are saved it is the power of God" (1 Cor.1:18).

Sir Robert refers to this verse and then says:

" 'THE preaching of the cross.' It is on this the great truth of grace depends. Not the death of Christ merely, but 'the cross.'" [1]

Anderson says that the death of the Lord Jesus cannot be separated from the Cross, especially the circumstances of that death:

"The doctrine of the 'death' of Christ, if separated from 'the cross,' leaves human nature still a standing ground. It is consistent with creature claims and class privileges. Sinners of the better sort can accept it, and be raised morally and intellectually by it. But the preaching of the cross is 'the axe laid to the root of the tree,' the death-blow to human nature on every ground and in every guise. It is not merely that Christ has died - the great fact on which redemption depends; but that that death has been brought about in a way and by means which manifest and prove not only the boundless and causeless love of God to man, but also the wanton and relentless enmity of man to God; that that death, while it has made it possible for God, in grace, to save the guiltiest and worst of Adam's race, has made it impossible, even with God, that the worthiest and best could be saved except in grace. It has measured out the moral distance between God and man, and has left them as far asunder as the throne of heaven and the gate of hell." [2]

Anderson says that in the early church there were many who perverted the gospel in order "to make it attractive to their hearers":

"Even in Paul's day 'the many' were but hucksters of the Word of God. Their aim was to make their wares acceptable, to secure a trade, as it were, and so they sought popularity and an apparent success by corrupting the gospel to make it attractive to their hearers." [3]

Here is the verse to which Anderson makes reference:

"For we are not as many, which corrupt the word of God: but as of sincerity, but as of God, in the sight of God speak we in Christ" (2 Cor.2:17).

The primary meaning of the Greek word translated "corrupt" is *"to retail, to peddle."* The secondary meaning is given here:

"To corrupt, to adulterate; peddlers were in the habit of adulterating their commodities for the sake of gain." [4]

Anderson describes how the gospel was being corrupted to make it attractive to its hearers:

"A gospel that points to the death of Christ in proof of God's high estimate of man, and then turns the doctrine of that death into a syllogism, so that men, in no way losing self-respect, can calmly reason out their right to blessing by it, will give no offence to any one, nor be branded as foolishness. Such a gospel pays due deference to human nature, and satisfies man's sense of need without hurting in the least his pride." [5]

Continuing on this theme Sir Robert says:

"Redemption as preached by 'the many' in Apostolic days brought no persecution, because it left man a platform on which 'to make a fair show in the flesh.' But the cross set aside the flesh altogether. If the death of Christ be preached as a means of salvation, not for lost sinners, but for the pious and devout, where is

the offence? But the cross comes in with its mighty power to bring low as well as to exalt, for it exalts none but those whom first it humbles. It calls upon the pious worshipper, if indeed he would have blessing, to come out from the shrine in which he trusts, and take his place in the market square beside the outcast and the vile. It tells the 'earnest seeker' and the 'anxious inquirer,' that by their efforts they are only struggling out of the pit where alone grace can reach them. It proclaims to the worthy 'communicant' of blameless life, whose mind is a treasury of orthodox doctrines, and whose ways are a pattern of all good, that he must come down and stand beside the drunkard and the harlot, there to receive salvation from the grace of God to the glory of God." [6]

Anderson says that the Cross is the result of man's philosophy, power and religion:

"The cross has shut man up to grace or judgment. It has broken down all 'partition walls,' and left a world of naked sinners trembling on the brink of hell. Every effort to recover themselves is but a denial of their doom, and a denial too of the grace of God, which stoops to bring them blessing where they are and as they are. The cross of Christ is the test and touch-stone of all things. Man's philosophy, man's power, man's religion - behold their work, the Christ of God upon a gallows!" [7]

Sir Robert says that it is this "preaching of the Cross" which changes men's hearts:

"It is one thing to master Christianity ; it is quite another thing to be mastered by it. And it is the cross that attracts and conquers. The cross, not as an easy way of pardon for the sinner, not as a 'plan of salvation,' but as a fact and a revelation to change a heartless worldling into an adoring worshipper. The cross, not as the ruling factor in the equation of man's redemption, but as a display of the love and righteousness and wrath of God, and the sin of man, to subdue the hardest heart, and change the whole current of the most selfish and ungodly life. To faith the unseen is real; and to those who believe in the cross, 'Jesus Christ has been openly set forth crucified before their eyes.' They have

seen that marred and agonised face. They have been witnesses to the reproach that broke His heart, the scorn, the derision, and the hate, of all the attendant throng. They have heard 'Emmanuel's orphan cry' when forsaken of His God. And in gazing thus upon that scene their inmost being has sustained a mighty change. Till yesterday, the world and self ensnared their hearts, and filled the whole horizon of their lives. But now the cross has become a power to divorce themselves from self, and to separate them from that world which crucified their Lord. O for power so to preach the cross of Christ that it shall become a reality to all, whether they accept it or despise it: that men who never were conscious of a doubt, because they never really 'believed,' shall see what priests and soldiers saw, and the rabble crowd that mocked His agonies, and seeing, shall exclaim, 'It is impossible that this can be the Son of God!' that some again shall see what John and Mary witnessed, and gazing, shall cry out, with broken hearts, in mingled love and grief, 'My God, was this for me!' and turn to live devoted lives for Him who died and rose again." [8]

Those who truly understand the "preaching of the Cross" will indeed *"turn to live devoted lives for Him who died and rose again."*

While it is of the utmost importance to understand that the Cross speaks of *"the shame and the contempt of men poured out without measure upon Him who died"* Sir Robert says that we should also gaze upon the triumphs of the Cross:

"Just as Israel stood on the wilderness side of the sea, and saw Pharaoh and his hosts in death upon the shore, it is ours to gaze upon the triumphs of the cross. God there has mastered sin, abolished death, and destroyed him who had the power of death. God has become our Saviour. Our trust is not in His mercy, but in Himself. Not in divine attributes, but in the living God. 'God is for us'; the Father is for us; the Son is for us; the Holy Ghost is for us. It is God who justifies; it is Christ that died; and the Holy Ghost has come down to be a witness to us of the work of Christ, and of the place that work has given us as sons in the Father's house. 'Behold, God is my salvation; I will trust and not

be afraid: for the Lord JEHOVAH is my strength and my song;
He also is become my salvation.' " ⁹

NOTES

1. Sir Robert Anderson, *The Gospel And Its Ministry*, 24.

2. *Ibid.,* 24-25.

3. *Ibid.,* 27.

4. Joseph Henry Thayer, *A Greek-English Lexicon of the New Testament*, 324.

5. Sir Robert Anderson, *The Gospel And Its Ministry*, 27.

6. *Ibid.,* 30.

7. *Ibid.,* 26.

8. *Ibid.,* 34-35.

9. Sir Robert Anderson, *The Gospel And Its Ministry*, 19-20.

The author encourages questions, comments and edifying discussion. Please contact him via email: jerryshugart2@yahoo.com

www.ingramcontent.com/pod-product-compliance
Lightning Source LLC
Chambersburg PA
CBHW021228090426
42740CB00006B/435